To Mike —
Christmas 1990
Kit

THE GRAND PASSAGE

THE GRAND PASSAGE

A Chronicle of North American Waterfowling

Illustrated With
Watercolor Paintings
and
Original Etchings
by

HERB BOOTH

COUNTRYSPORT PRESS
Traverse City, Michigan

© 1990 by Countrysport, Inc.

Published by Countrysport, Inc., P.O. Box 1856, Traverse City, MI 49685

All rights reserved, including the right to reproduce this book or portions thereof in any form or by any means, electronic or mechanical, including photocopying, recording, or by any information storage and retrieval system, without the permission in writing from the publisher. All inquiries should be addressed to: Countrysport Inc., P.O. Box 1856, Traverse City, MI 49685

Printed in the United States of America

Library of Congress Catalog Card Number: 89-81947

ISBN 0-924357-10-X   Trade Edition
ISBN 0-924357-13-4   Deluxe Edition

Dedication

*To the generations of waterfowlers yet unborn,
that they may inherit the opportunity
to enjoy the grandest of sport.*

Contents

Introduction ix
   by The Authors

An Introduction To Sporting Etchings and Drypoints:
The Frank Benson Tradition 13
   by John Talbot Ordeman

CHAPTER ONE
   Memories of Divers 31
      by Robert Elman

CHAPTER TWO
   Distant Wings 47
      by Richard S. Grozik

CHAPTER THREE
   Retriever Tribulations 63
      by Bobby George, Jr.

CHAPTER FOUR
   Gunning the Grand Passage 79
      by Michael McIntosh

CHAPTER FIVE
   Canadian Reflections 107
      by Bill McClure

CHAPTER SIX
   Waterfowling Abroad: The International Experience 123
      by Stuart Williams

CHAPTER SEVEN
   The Other Side of Sport 139
      by Terry Wieland

CHAPTER EIGHT
   The Wild Goose 155
      by Gene Hill

Watercolor Paintings And Full-Page Etchings by Herb Booth

PAINTINGS

    Diver Island — Bluebills 32

    Flooded Timber — Mallards 48

    Back Door Woodies 64

    Pit Blind 80

    Specklebellies in the Spread 96

    Canada Honkers 112

    Teal & Tree Ducks 128

    Pintails High 144

ETCHINGS

    The Old Dock 28

    Dawn 53

    Seasoned Veteran 71

    Bay Blind 76

    Opening Day 89

    Double-Ender 117

    Game Parade 131

    American Classics 151

    Reconnaissance 157

Introduction

The Grand Passage has long stood for the great migrations of ducks and geese from their nesting grounds in the North to the wintering grounds of the South. It is the period when they are foremost in the thoughts of those who seek them – waterfowlers.

And as waterfowling moves into the last decade of this century, The Grand Passage also serves as a metaphor for the passing of waterfowling into a new era, the Age of Appreciation.

The days of the huge bags in North America are gone; even if they were still possible, a new waterfowling ethic has taken hold where the experience – not the size of the bag – is the measuring stick by which a hunt is judged.

The North American waterfowler is drawn to the great waters that hold the diving ducks; to the potholes, honey holes, plains, and prairies that hold the dabblers; to the fields and marshes that speak to the Canada, snow, and white-front geese. Always, he is drawn.

But not for the shooting alone, although that's a part of it, but for the joy of having hunted – of having been there – and to be better for it. He recognizes with each passing season that he is but a caretaker of a vast resource, one that comes, in turn, to depend upon him more at those same seasons pass.

For it is only through our ability to care, to appreciate, and to savor the wonder of The Grand Passage that we can ensure it will continue.

The Authors

The Grand Passage *is illustrated with water-color paintings and with etchings by sporting artist Herb Booth of Texas. This latter medium, sporting etchings, is a time-consuming labor of love by the artist, and is one of the older, traditional forms of artistic expression.*

No author is better able to give an overview of this method than John Talbot Ordeman. He is Headmaster of Broadwater Academy on Virginia's Eastern Shore, and the author of three books on etching and drypoint art: Frank W. Benson: Master of the Sporting Print; William Schaldach: Artist/Author/Sportsman; *and* To Keep a Tryst with the Dawn: An Appreciation of Roland Clark.

An Introduction To Sporting Etchings and Drypoints: The Frank Benson Tradition

by John Talbot Ordeman

Following established British tradition, American painters of the nineteenth and twentieth centuries took the genre of the formal bird study as their natural inheritance. Thomas Bewick's drawings for his *History of British Birds*, published in 1797, were the models for the works of John James Audubon, for Audubon's follower, Louis Agassiz Fuertes, and, in our time, for Roger Tory Peterson.

The pictures by these Americans, paintings reproduced in color, first by the application of watercolors to engravings and later by various photolithographic processes, are essentially ornithological studies. The subjects are generally posed, standing against a background depicting their habitat to have their portraits painted. Their poses may indicate activity – eating, preening, feeding their young, fighting – but these activities lack a sense of motion. Even when the birds are flying, they appear to be marvels of taxidermy suspended on wires.

The artists were ornithologists working with meticulous attention to detail to earn the approval of fellow naturalists. This is the tradition inherited from the British, and the artists who worked in this tradition produced pictures notable for artistic quality as well as scientific accuracy. The works produced by these bird portraitists, however, did not capture the essence of their subjects, for a bird in flight is not a static creature.

The extraordinary achievement of conveying the essence of birds – in particular, of waterfowl – in the visual arts is generally credited to an exceptionally talented and versatile artist, Frank W. Benson.

A classically trained draftsman, oil painter, and watercolorist, Frank Benson won more cash prizes, medals, and other honors than any other American artist in the early years of the twentieth century. An academician of the National Academy, a founding member of the distinguished group of impressionists known as The Ten, he could take pride in the fact that his pictures hung in the permanent collections of most of the nation's most prestigious museums.

In 1912, at the age of fifty, he began to experiment with the engraving medium called *intaglio*, something he did solely for relaxation and the pleasure of trying something new. He occasionally gave prints to friends, but he apparently had no intention of publishing an edition of prints for sale at that time. Three years later, however, without realizing the significance of a spur-of-the-moment decision, he placed some etchings and drypoints in an exhibition of his paintings at the Guild of Boston Artists. He was greatly surprised to find that these pictures, particularly those depicting flying ducks, sold well and that there was a pressing demand for additional prints. Frank Benson's good friend, the noted etcher Samuel Chamberlain, recalled the reaction of those who attended the exhibition and Mr. Benson's response:

Frank Benson

"Visitors to the exhibition liked the portraits and the hunting scenes, but above all they liked his birds. Their reaction to etchings of ducks in flight was not merely favorable, it was electric. Quite by accident a new, crystal-clear note in etching had been rung...

"This first startling success had a stimulating effect on the etcher who, as a painter, had known great triumphs. The year 1915 saw him become a very active and enthusiastic print maker."

Etching was a popular medium at that time, and when Frank Benson began his experiments with the etching needle and the drypoint burin in the second decade of this century, he could study works in the intaglio medium by some of the world's foremost artists, his contemporaries and those of the previous generations: Goya, Delacroix, Renoir, Manet, Van Gogh, Cezanne, Turner, Whistler, Picasso, Klee, and Matisse.

In a zealous burst of creative energy, Mr. Benson produced fifty-two etchings and drypoints in 1915. He had been making intaglio prints for only two years when Adam Paff compiled and published a catalogue raisonne, *Etchings and Drypoints of Frank W. Benson*, which would eventually run to five volumes covering his total output of 355 prints produced over a period of three decades.

The popular appeal of Mr. Benson's works was such that an edition, usually 150 prints, was often sold out before actual release, for many collectors subscribed through standing orders with his dealers. Sportsmen marveled at these pictures, for the artist saw ducks and geese as they did. The birds in Mr. Benson's prints are miraculously alive, and they live in the natural world. Mr. Benson explained, "I try to make them part of the landscape in which they occur, rather than to describe them as specimens. What I enjoy about them is their *wildness*." "His plates succeed in creating the atmosphere of wildfowl haunts in prints of fine composition," wrote a fellow artist who was also a waterfowler. "Action blends with the scene to build the picture so dear to the gunner's memory."

Waterfowlers who sensed that only a fellow sportsman who had spent many hours in blinds could draw flying ducks as Frank Benson did were, of course, correct in their surmise; from his youth,

Frank Benson had been an ardent duck hunter who had spent thousands of hours observing birds in flight. He knew their every movement, and he could render them with never a false stroke of the drypointist's and etcher's tools.

"Benson's great achievement is that he created something that did not exist before," wrote Childe Reece, an authoritative art historian in the mid-1930s. "Not only did he invent, one might say, the sporting etching, but he gave it form." Another critic, who calls Mr. Benson "the originator of the American sporting etching," states that Mr. Benson gave it "form, continuity of line and an American individuality" and lay "the cornerstone to the coherent and national school."

Having learned the art of intaglio printmaking by trial and error, working as an amateur solely for the satisfaction of mastering the new media, Frank Benson made extraordinary progress, becoming in a very brief time an accomplished etcher and drypointist.

In an essay entitled "What Is an Etching?" Mr. Benson, for years a teacher of drawing and painting who enjoyed sharing his knowledge with students, explained the basic techniques of etching and drypoint as he practiced them. As he performed himself all of the tasks required to produce intaglio prints – from creating the design, through operating the press, to pulling the completed print from the plate – he could speak with experience and authority, to guide young artists along paths he had discovered as a lone explorer.

"What Is an Etching?"
by Frank W. Benson

An *Etching* is an engraving made upon a plate of copper, zinc, or other metal by the use of nitric acid or some other mordant.

The print made on paper from the etched plate is print or proof, though such a print is usually called an etching.

The *Plate* is prepared for etching by covering it thinly and evenly, while heated, with a composition of wax and asphaltum which when cold becomes firm enough to resist handling, but gives the least possible resistance to the needle used in tracing the necessary lines on the copper. The object is to uncover the copper without scratching it, leaving the exposed metal to be bitten by the acid.

The *Mordant*, or agent for biting the lines in the plate, is most commonly nitric acid. This acid is favored because its action is made visible by the accumulation of green bubbles along the lines of the work, giving a measure of the amount of work accomplished. It has its drawbacks from danger of handling and disagreeable fumes, and these are absent in the use of ferric chloride which, however, bites the line invisibly. Ferric chloride is dark in color, and hides the lines, and the work that it does in the plate must be judged by time or by frequent washing and drying of the plate for examination.

Having grounded the plate, as covering it with wax is called, it is smoked over the flame of a candle to make the surface black, in order that the lines on the copper, traced by the needle, may be clearly seen. The design being made, the plate is lowered into a tray of acid which has been diluted with rather more than its own bulk of water. The experience of the etcher tells him when the lines which are to be most delicate have been sufficiently bitten. The plate is then washed in a tray of water, dried, and the part finished is covered with stopping out varnish – some quick-drying compound like shellac. Repeated baths in the acid result in a set of lines variously bitten, which make up, if successful, the intended picture.

But the lines are not only deeper as the biting goes on; they also become wider, and this brings up the question of the use of various mordants, since nitric acid widens the lines more than ferric chloride, and the latter, more than Dutch mordant, which is composed of muriatic acid and chlorate of potash. Consequently the etcher often makes use of different mordants in the production of an etched plate. Another way of producing this decided variety in the width of lines is by using points of various thickness, grinding the steel so that a line may be drawn on the plate as wide as that of a soft lead pencil.

One of the greatest difficulties to the beginner is the fact that after the plate has been partly etched, it practically disappears as a picture. The etcher is working with faith in his intention which was at first shown in the plate but which has disappeared, in patches, if not completely. In a bath of ferric chloride it cannot be seen at all – the length of the immersion is timed by the clock, ruled by previous experience. In general, the light lines are bitten in three minutes or less, according to the strength of the mordant used. For it must be understood that etching if followed seriously leads to many experiments, and every etcher of long standing does it in his own way. He may vary the strength of the acid, so that his light lines require ten minutes when with stronger acid they would be done in three. He finds that a slowly bitten line is cleaner cut than one more quickly made with a stronger acid. So any figures that I give as to strength of acid used may be varied.

When one takes a pencil and begins drawing on paper, he can easily change the whole plan of the drawing. He can rub out his lines and masses of shadow and change their position almost at will. The contrast is felt at once when he takes a copper plate in hand to make an etching. A line made is practically irrevocable. Besides this, the lines are all alike or nearly so. The final and necessary difference must be made by the acid instead of by the pressure of the hand holding the pencil. So the whole plan of work must be formed beforehand; and the final result will be seen only when, after the successive bitings of the plate, washings and dryings, the whole covering of the plate, ground and stopping out varnish, is cleaned off with turpentine or gasoline, and alcohol if shellac is used. Then on the bright copper, the design is seen in dark lines. Too often there is seen a sprinkling of dots that will print as dark points – the result of grains of dust in the ground which have been eaten away by the acid, resulting in pits in the plate unsuspected by the etcher. With nitric acid these are seen, if numerous, before they become deep, but with the other mordants they sometimes spoil the plate. If in a clear space they can be scraped out with much labor and the plate repolished.

The method I have described is the old, regular, traditional way of making an etching. But it can be and is, varied in a hundred ways to gain certain ends. For example, the obvious difficulty of stopping out some lines in the drawing and at the same time leaving others close to them to receive further biting has led some etchers to make only a part of the drawing on the plate at first – perhaps only the lines that were to be the strongest. These having been bitten, the next in force are added and so on till the last and finest set are added. Using this method, none of the lines are covered at any time, but it requires a well formed plan to make a success. Other etchers do not use the tray of acid at all but simply put a little pool of acid or other mordant on the part of the plate which is to receive the strongest biting, then by successive stages lead the mordant to the rest of the lines. If after cleaning the plate, the result looks hopeful the etcher proceeds to "prove" the plate. Though the design can be clearly seen now on the copper, the real success can only be told when it is printed in black lines on white.

In preparation for proving, sheets of handmade paper have been soaked in water and are waiting between damp blotters to be used in proving the plate. The press in which this is done has an iron table running between heavy iron rollers which are actuated by a big wheel some five feet in diameter. The pressure used is indicated by the size of this wheel, and the printer often uses not only his hands but a foot as well in putting a plate through the press. The plate is now heated about as hot as can comfortably be handled, and thick ink is rubbed into the lines and all over the plate with a dabber. The ink is as thick as honey. It is then wiped off with cloths until the design begins to be seen, the lines of course

An Introduction to Sporting Etchings and Drypoints

holding the ink while the surface begins to be clean. The wiping, which is the real scientific part of printing, is completed with a palm of the hand, and a great variety of results can be had from the same plate by different methods of wiping.

The plate is now laid face upward on the bed of the press, which runs between the rollers, the damp paper is placed upon it, and over all are laid three or four press blankets of fine felted wool. The whole being pressed through the rollers, the blankets force the paper into the inked lines of the plate, and when the blankets are lifted and the paper peeled from the plate, the real result of the etching is seen and not till then.

Fine papers of various sorts are sought by the etcher for printing, and many sorts are used, but only handmade papers – Dutch, Japanese, French, and Italian – will give perfect results in plate finishing. The whole process from the bare plate to the finished print is full of fascinating possibilities and possible failures.

The *Dry Point* is a free-hand engraving made upon a plate of copper or zinc with a needle or other sharp tool of steel. Dry points are often called etchings, which they are not, for, as I have said, an etching is an engraving made with acid.

To make a dry point one simply takes a clean copper plate and a needle set in a strong handle, or a dentist's tool ground to a sharp point, and scratches the design on the copper. The variation in effect is made by the varying depth of the lines as in an etching, and the making of the heavier lines requires considerable strength of hand. But the difference in appearance between an etching and a dry point is very evident; and this is caused by the fact that the tool used not only cuts a furrow but throws up a ridge parallel to it, and this ridge holds ink behind it when the plate is wiped. It results that the dry point plate is usually more velvety in appearance and softer in quality than one which is etched.

Since the plate depends for its richness of dark lines upon the ridge thrown up by the needle, and since this ridge wears off quickly under the wear of wiping the plate, it is not possible to print a very large number of proofs from a dry point plate. But there is a process called "steel-facing" which adds much to its life. This consists in hanging the plate in an electric bath and coating it with a very fine film or steel – so fine that though it penetrates into every line, and covers the surface, it does not perceptibly affect the strength of the print.

In the case of an etched plate from which many proofs are to be taken, this steel-facing can be renewed as often as it wears through to the copper, but in the case of a dry point plate, when the ridges between the lines are worn, the plate no longer will print well. By steel-facing, an etched plate may be printed thousands of times. A dry point will rarely yield two hundred proofs; often not half of that.

There are many interesting side-paths connected with the art of etching – methods of work and varieties of effect to be produced that would interest anyone who wanted to go deeply into the processes. For these matters of detail it is best to go to a book where one can dwell on such matters of interest and compare them. Maxime Lalanne's *Treatise on Etching* is one of the best and has given many a young etcher all the technical help he needs to send him on his way. An English translation was made by S. R. Koehler. There are many other good books on the subject, old and new, and one who takes the trouble to read them may find them interesting in themselves. They will surely result in a deeper interest in etchings and dry points.

The critical and commercial success that had greeted Frank Benson's early prints of waterfowl inspired others to take up the tools of the intaglio artist. Like Mr. Benson, they were essentially self-taught, relying on their study of the works of other artists, Mr. Benson in particular, employing trial and error to develop their skill.

First, and perhaps foremost, among those who took the path Frank Benson had blazed was Roland Clark, who created his first intaglio print in 1919. Mr. Clark had been a painter of sporting subjects as well as a writer of stories and essays for sporting publications for two decades when he first began, at the suggestion of his principal dealer in New York, to work on copper plate with the drypointist's burin.

A deft draftsman with a sure, strong hand, Roland Clark, from the first, produced prints that were remarkably competent; and he published a small print of wood ducks after only a few months of experimentation. He then produced nineteen prints in 1920, after which he averaged ten to twelve drypoints a year for the next decade, and about half that number each year through the 1930s and into the 1940s. A few of Mr. Clark's prints depict upland game birds; however, ducks, shorebirds, and geese were his standard subjects. Although he worked exclusively in the drypoint medium, Roland Clark, rather inexplicably, always referred to his intaglio prints as etchings, and a book of his drypoints The Derrydale Press published in 1937 was titled *Roland Clark's Etchings*.

Like Frank Benson, Roland Clark had spent a lifetime as a hunter of ducks, and sportsmen know instinctively that the artist whose works they so admired was one of them.

The third artist who was to make a name for himself as a maker of intaglio sporting prints was Richard E. Bishop. Unlike Frank Benson and Roland Clark, Mr. Bishop was not an established artist when he began to make prints in 1920. He was employed as a mechanical engineer, running a rolling mill, when he used the reverse side of a discarded wedding invitation, engraving plate, and a phonograph needle to make his first etching. He continued to play with the etcher's tools and eventually took instruction in design and etching techniques.

A critic reviewing a 1932 exhibition of Richard Bishop's work wrote, "The etchings make a striking group...Sportsmen and collectors will appreciate them, for they are based on thorough knowledge of bird life and are interpreted with skill and vividness.

Roland Clark

The thrill of suspense the hunter feels is easily seen in various examples of ducks in graceful flight over marshes."

In 1924, Mr. Bishop won an award for his print "Canada Geese," which he offered for sale in an edition of 65; and his career as a professional artist was launched, a career that would stretch over a half-century. After spending several years developing his skills as an etcher, Mr. Bishop turned to the more difficult medium of drypoint, which he came to prefer because it enables the artist to achieve a broader range of visual effects.

A decade after he began his printmaking, Mr. Bishop's work had established him as a sporting artist of the first rank. A critic wrote: "Bishop's work can be compared to only one other American etcher, the older, more versatile artist, Frank W. Benson. Yet Bishop manages to get into his pictures more color value, better atmosphere effects, and greater delicacy of line than the former New England artist." Tom Davis recently noted, "Delicacy is indeed the hallmark of Bishop's mature style. The images, which are strong and clean and incisive, retain a remarkable quality. Only after he had established himself as an etcher and drypointist did Mr. Bishop take formal instruction in painting techniques and begin to build his reputation as a painter in oils and watercolors, a reputation now equal to his reputation as a printmaker.

Churchill Ettinger, a popular and prolific etcher and drypointist specializing in waterfowl subjects, was a younger contemporary of The Big Three – Benson of Boston, Clark of New York, and Bishop of Philadelphia.

Aiden Lassell Ripley was a sportsman/artist, trained in the Benson tradition in Boston. Known primarily for his prints and paintings of upland game shooting scenes, Mr. Ripley demonstrated his ability to depict waterfowl in a number of prints, including the 1942 duck stamp design, "American Widgeon."

Among other American artists who produced etchings and drypoints of waterfowl in the fourth and fifth decades of the twentieth century – the Golden Age of the sporting etching –were Hans Klieber, Lynn Bogue Hunt, Marquerite Kirmse. Carl Rungius and William Schaldach, noted sporting etchers of this period, did not choose waterfowl as their subjects.

THE GRAND PASSAGE

An extraordinary boost to collector interest in wildfowl art was an unexpected consequence of the institution of a tax levied on waterfowl hunters. When the Federal government adopted Ding Darling's suggestion that all hunters of ducks and geese be required to buy a stamp to be affixed to their state hunting licenses to provide funds for conservation projects, everyone realized that waterfowl would benefit through the creation and preservation of breeding grounds and resting areas. No one, however, anticipated just how much wildlife artists would ultimately benefit.

Beginning in 1936 with the third duck stamp design, based on Richard Bishop's etching "Coming In," the drawing, print, or painting chosen each year as the duck stamp design has been published as an original limited edition print. The artists who had created the first and second designs, Ding Darling and Frank Benson, were prevailed upon in later years to produce prints of their designs as well to accommodate sportsmen who wanted a complete set of the prints. An increasing number of collectors created a demand which has caused the prices of prints of the earlier designs to rise rapidly and has afforded artists an opportunity to produce multiple editions of their designs.

The first thirty-six of these duck stamp prints were original black-and-white etchings, drypoints, or stone lithographs, each of which, with the exception of Mr. Bishop's and Mr. Ripley's designs, was produced in a relatively small edition. Since 1970, however – with the single exception of Maynard Reece's 1971 "Cinnamon Teal," which was hand-colored – all of the prints have been full-color photolithographic reproductions of paintings. Collectors had demonstrated a preference for large, colorful pictures; artists and dealers were eager to supply the sort of print that the public would buy.

The notable success of the Federal stamp program encouraged the states positioned along the migratory bird flyways to institute waterfowl stamp programs of their own, and artists now have many opportunities to enter stamp design contests and, if they win, to market prints of their designs to collectors.

Etchings and drypoints – small linear pictures in black and white – did not have the same broad appeal as the colorful photolithographs. The intaglio media, furthermore, could not produce the number of original prints sufficient to meet the demand of the collectors of duck stamp prints, a group that has come to be numbered

Richard Bishop

Herb Booth

by tens of thousands. Interest in sporting art was never greater than in the past two decades, but this interest has not been reflected in a demand for intaglio prints.

About a decade ago I addressed this matter in a monograph on Frank W. Benson: "Many collector's regret the passing of artists' interest in meeting the demands and accepting the challenge of the intaglio media." Today I am able to write that those of us who are interested in sporting art may rejoice that there are, among the present generation of sporting artists, some who have been working to develop printmaking skills.

David Hagerbaumer, a premier painter of waterfowl, upland game birds and hunting scenes, took up etching in 1981 and produced a set of eight etchings, with each edition limited to ninety prints, the number Mr. Hagerbaumer has chosen for each of his twelve subsequent editions as well. Four hand-colored etchings were issued in 1984, the coloring being done by Mr. Hagerbaumer himself or by his daughter, Cindy.

Mr. Hagerbaumer has etched half a dozen more plates, which are complete sporting scenes – the triad of hunter, dog, and bird in the tradition of the eighteenth century English artist Henry Alken as followed by Arthur Fitzwilliam Tait, Currier and Ives' artist, A.B. Frost and a good many contemporary artists, including Mr. Hagerbaumer.

A younger contemporary of David Hagerbaumer's, who has also taken up etching after having established a reputation as an outstanding painter of sporting scenes, is Herb Booth. Mr. Booth, like his predecessors whose work he has admired and studied, is essentially self-taught as a printmaker. His first productions, some of which serve as illustrations in this book, demonstrate more than mere promise.

Among others who are currently depicting ducks and geese in etchings and drypoints are Dave Chapple, Doug Allen, James Harvey Johnson, Paul Niemiec, and Al Barker. Intaglio printmaking is apparently undergoing a revival among American sporting artists, and we may be on the verge of another Golden Age.

The Frank Benson tradition in the genre of sporting etchings and dry points lives on.

The history of waterfowling is rooted in diver duck shooting: market gunning, punt guns, the Eastern Shore, storms on Chesapeake Bay. These are the fabric of our gunning culture and heritage.

And the great rafts of birds we associate with big water – the redheads and canvasbacks and bluebills and broadbills and the rest – and the life of gunning they spawned are with us still, muted by time, but there nonetheless.

One who is able to paint in words this varied picture of sport is Bob Elman. A book author many times over, magazine editor, avid waterfowler, and sporting historian, Bob still lives near the Eastern Shore that he loves so well.

CHAPTER ONE

Memories of Divers

by
Robert Elman

During my early adolescence – or "first adolescence," as my wife refers to it – I lived in a New Jersey town skirted by farmland, farm ponds, and an abundance of small streams. To me, the "duck" meant mallard, and a sizable rig of decoys numbered a dozen. The habitat attracted only dabbling ducks, and not many species of those. I saw a few high-flying sprig (although years passed before I ever had a chance to bag one), and occasionally in the evening or when I skipped school to meet my hunting and getting-into-trouble pal, Bobby Malvern, down at the river, I actually saw woodies back in those years when the wood duck was almost an endangered species.

In brief, I was raised on puddle ducks, mergansers, and Canada geese and didn't know much about them or any other waterfowl. Once, Bobby pointed out a sloping column of maybe half a dozen black ducks that refused to give our decoys a nod, and I didn't know enough to feel frustrated. They looked like big, dark mallard hens to me.

Diver Island – Bluebills
From The North American Wingshooting Portfolio
Countrysport Press

I'd read Ray Holland, Van Campen Heilner, Eugene Connett, Raymond Camp, and other illustrious gunning writers; I devoured sporting books and magazines. Often the writers sang paeans to diving ducks on big waters. Yet their stories for all the solid hunting wisdom in them, remained unreal to me, like who-done-its and Westerns. I just didn't know.

I was almost grown when at last I visited Maryland's Eastern Shore and saw a stool of more than eighty bluebill decoys and saw, too, my first live bluebills and redheads and cans, rafts of them on the water enormously outnumbering that meager stool, crowds and clouds of them in the sky. It was a benumbing revelation, a duck hunter's equivalent of getting religion, suddenly being born again. So *that's* what those writers were talking about. My God, they weren't exaggerating, they were telling the damn truth! To this day, I believe I might have been able to hit at least one of the first four scaup I fired at, had I not been so awe-stricken.

The analogy with religion isn't offered facetiously or disrespectfully. Watching a mauve sunrise beginning to glow over a salt-marsh blind near Jersey's Barnegat Bay, I've felt as close to eternal verities as I ever have while sitting in a pew, and the birds were choir enough for me.

Once I had experienced the sights and sounds – and yes, the shooting – associated with divers, I began to understand the kind of sporting literature that had formerly seemed mere fantasy. Mallards had been my first love and would forever delight me; I knew that, but now I also knew that there's room in life for more than one love. Times, locales, conditions change mightily, sometimes depressingly, yet the waterfowler or any other communicant of the natural world recognizes unchanging, universal wonders. Nelson Bryant spoke for all of us in *The Wildfowler's World*:

> *One could be huddled on the bare, dark rocks of the Thimble Islands off Connecticut in Long Island Sound as a December wind cuts deep, waiting for scaup to come to the seventy-five or hundred decoys...One could be crouched in a wild-rose thicket on Martha's Vineyard as a northeast gale whirls stinging sand along the beach...or on a backwater of the Mississippi or Missouri...or on one*

of the storied Eastern coastal bays or sounds – the Chesapeake, Currituck, Albemarle, Pamlico.

Beside the sea or away from it, whether by lake, bay, pond, river, or inland marsh, one hides, or remains motionless, and waits...Whatever the place, the magic is the same, and for a little while man forgets his mundane duties and enters the primitive world of the hunter, responding to an urge that is as valid as the desire to love a woman or beget a child.

When Nels wrote that in 1973, he was responding to the same exultation described by Roland Clark in *Gunner's Dawn* almost forty years earlier: "Is there anything quite like a winter morning – with a rose light breaking in the east and dark lines of ducks in silhouette against the far-flung screen?" Both were celebrating the exultation recorded by sensitive wildfowling writers for the last couple of centuries and certain to be recorded by others in the century about to dawn.

Early experiences, when a particular kind of hunting is still new and much is to be learned, are among the experiences most treasured. How sharply I remember a cold, black morning two decades ago when a Maryland friend took me along for broadbills – greater scaup. I believe it was November, and good numbers of broadies had been arriving. I held the light while my friend Dave hunched over the trailer hitch and winch, launching his flat-bottomed sixteen-footer. I must have been a hindrance then and afterward, for I also remember stumbling over bushel baskets of decoys.

Dave went forward and knelt at the steering wheel, a duck hunter's duck hunter, seemingly impervious to icy spray, and we rolled against a steady chop where the river emptied into Fishing Bay. Several miles down the windward side, at a ribbon point of public marshland, we set out the blocks in front of a slat-and-rush blind. Near the blind and slightly to the right we put out a dozen honker decoys. Farther out and to the left we set about two dozen canvasback decoys and some scaup, and finally we trailed a few black duck blocks on calmer water near an undercut bank – not a huge traditional rig, but I knew it would suffice because I knew Dave had been hunting divers so long and so successfully that he understood a duck's desires as thoroughly as any duck could.

It was Dave, not I, who expressed a kind of fatalism that would strike the uninitiated as pessimistic: "Wind's in our faces. The birds'll have a hell of a time coming into this rig, but this is the blind we've got to use and those are the breaks. Might as well relax and have some coffee."

False dawn dissolved into a cloudless, birdless sky, and we were a long time waiting. We were cold but content, watching red-winged blackbirds dart into the tall grasses behind us, a heron hover momentarily above the Canada decoys, and several loons flit over the water. The loons especially delighted me, as I associated them with other regions I'd hunted and fished – Vermont, Minnesota – and didn't realize they frequented this part of the country or this coastal habitat. A merganser passed over the blind, returned, and came low across us on its third pass. Tempted though I was, I sat still. Unlike many gunners of my generation, I don't regard mergansers as trash, but to kill one while waiting and praying for bluebills would be close to a premature admission of defeat.

I was on the edge of drowsing when Dave whispered, "Broadbills," and hunched down, cupping his hands and purring like a cat but louder. It's not hard to use a wooden call to mimic the loud, discordant, repetitive caw of scaup in flight, though the sound is quite similar to the alarm call of lesser scaup and can flare birds instead of enticing them if it isn't used judiciously and skillfully. Like many traditional bluebill hunters, Dave let his duck call dangle on its lanyard while he used his mouth and cupped hand to emit a mellow growl: "*b-b-b-r-r-r-r-r-r, b-b-r-r-rur.*"

The birds came in high, a wavering, almost shapeless wedge, but I'm certain they heard the call in spite of the wind. The wedge compacted itself into what looked like a ball, and then the ball came apart – a phenomenon some of the old Eastern Shore guides used to call "smoking the sky." As they approached the rig, they bunched closer again, forming an expanding and contracting arc, as if strung on a gigantic invisible rubber band – and then dropped abruptly, very steeply, seeming to fall out of the sky. A magnificent sight, except that they came down just out of range, beyond the far side of our decoy spread, and bobbed contentedly on the swells.

Then a second flight came in, this one only thirty, maybe forty feet above the water, a hundred birds or more, and our hopes soared as high as the birds were low. But they joined the first flock and showed no inclination to rise again or paddle close enough for us to rise and flush them off the water. How tantalizing the situation was, how frustrating – how infuriating after the first half-hour. Such, quite often, is the nature of scaup, or broadbill, or bluebill, or blackhead, or raft duck or whatever else you may be tempted to call these ducks.

Dave purred, and purred again, and when the scaup ignored him he took off his hat and waved it gently, just above the blind. "They're curious little buggers, you know," he said. "The old-timers in some regions used to toll them in by running a small dog back and forth on the shore."

Having read about that, I felt hopeful, but the hat had no effect. Finally, he pulled a white handkerchief from his hip pocket and waved it. Several of the ducks spotted it, came a bit closer to investigate, then traded about near the outer fringe of our rig, suspicious but insufficiently curious. Dave pocketed the handkerchief and purred again, and several of the ducks swam right in among our decoys. In my wrists and ankles I felt that old familiar tingling sensation that comes to me with buck fever. "Now!" Dave said.

I'm one of the many duck hunters (more of them than will admit it) who is never fully ready for "Now!" Dave stood and swung as ducks skittered over the water, getting airborne. He bagged the two that were highest in the air, and I missed one twice even though its take-off gave me a better opportunity than the spring-loaded rise of a surprised mallard – a bird I was accustomed to jump-shooting.

Those were the days of lead shot, and No. 4s were popular for this kind of gunning for the obvious reason that they were efficient. But my two loads of No.4s threaded their way around the target to arc through the sky and somewhere far out there, drop harmlessly into the water. I had no further chance to disgrace myself that day. It didn't matter. I knew I was a confirmed idolater of diving ducks, and I have never had any wish to stray from the faith.

This prompts me to ponder both the attraction and the definition of divers. Neither consideration is as simple as it seemed to our forefathers. Ornithologists list five closely related *pochards*, or diving-duck species – canvasback, redhead, greater scaup, lesser scaup, and ringneck. Hunters sometimes are less precise in speaking of divers, because other species like the company of pochards. A man can tell you he went out for divers

Memories of Divers

today and managed to bag a couple, and then hold up a scaup and a baldpate. I'll return to that subject later.

Perhaps more intriguing is the question of why hunters are so beguiled by diving ducks. A major part of the attraction has always been the natural setting in which divers are most often hunted – big waters, sprawling marshlands, wide horizons, plenty of sky, and relative solitude even in this era of dwindling habitat.

Generally speaking, this kind of ecosystem (surprisingly, to casual observers) isn't as rich in waterfowl foods and protective cover as the environments more heavily frequented by many species of dabbling ducks. Divers rely to a far greater extent on aquatic foods, some of them deeply submerged, than on emergent vegetation and such easy pickings as corn, wheat, mast, wild millet, and so on. The second part of the canvasback's scientific name (*Aythya valisneria*) refers to its appetite for the wild celery, its favorite food in freshwater, and particularly the deeply submerged tips of the rootstocks; and the vernacular name "scaup" also indicates feeding habits and habitat. Whereas the redhead, canvasback, and ringneck (more aptly called ringbill in some regions) derive their common names from aspects of their appearance, the greater and lesser scaup derive theirs from an old Scottish term for an oyster or mussel bed, the same derivation as that of the succulent scallop. The supply of mollusks, eelgrass, wild celery, widgeongrass, pondweed, muskgrass, water lily, bulrush, arrowhead, and so on – this supply is not as great as once it was, and it has always demanded harder foraging than foods found on land and at the edges of tip-up shallows, but it is widespread. What's lacking in easy accessibility is made up in spacious habitat, which attracts wildfowlers as well as wildfowl.

Most divers historically have tended to decoy with an innocence occasionally suggesting a death wish, and ringnecks can be downright gullible, but this has changed somewhat in recent years, especially where hunting pressure is heavy. Though redheads may approach eagerly in the first week of the season, they need only a few lessons before they start to associate decoys with gunfire. Another attraction, therefore, is the very frustration I've described in connection with scaup: the unpredictability.

The related effort involved in bagging them is part of it, too. Assuming your boat is hidden or camouflaged and your blind isn't laughable, redheads and sometimes scaup and assuredly ringnecks may try to join your stool as if dropping in for a family reunion, but they won't be tempted by the half-dozen or dozen decoys that can draw mallards to a creek bend or little farm pond. When you've set out more than a hundred floaters and realize that there's no possibility of picking them up every evening at the end of shooting hours – that you'll have to leave them (where legal) and explain to the boss and the wife how often you must return to check on those decoys – you acquire a kind of dedication akin to obstinacy; this much effort, this much sacrifice must and will pay off.

Even the sounds of divers exert a peculiar attraction. When a big wedge of redheads comes in, you may hear the whir of the wind through their primaries, but it's the calls – the calls are the addiction. You can growl and mutter into your call to answer the squeaky quacks and rasps of redheads, and you can coax them closer by purring like a housecat, as you can with scaup, both greater and lesser. You can do it with ringnecks, too, though these ducks are less talkative than the others and, personally, I think it's a bit easier to get their attention by trilling into a wooden call than by relying on your vocal cords. Hen canvasbacks quack rather like mallards, but the drakes *peep* and *coo* and have an intriguing series of flight calls that might be described as grunting or growling punctuated by occasional hoarse croaks. It's all music, and a language eternally challenging, amusing, never fully learned.

There are differences of opinion about scaup as table fare – obviously depending on what they've been eating. But I've always found them to be somewhere between good enough and wonderful if prepared properly. Fat ringnecks are better. Redheads, in my experience, are equally fine, and canvasbacks are unsurpassed when they've been taken over freshwater where they've been feeding on wild celery.

If the aforementioned unpredictability and difficulties are a gift of spiritual retreat from our overmechanized lives, it must be admitted that a combination of fine eating and incredible abundance – totally predictable abundance – were major attractions in the era now recalled as the Golden Age. Certainly this was true along vast stretches of the Mississippi and Atlantic flyways. Freight-car loads of diving ducks were shipped to markets and restaurants east and west from the Mississippi region, west and north from the great Meccas of the Atlantic Flyway. By the turn of the century, business

was almost equally brisk along a great portion of the Pacific Coast and some parts of what we now call the Central flyway.

In *The Outlaw Gunner*, a marvelous little history of Eastern market shooting before and after it was prohibited, Harry Walsh reminds us of the halcyon Eastern Shore days when "a raft of nearly 2,000 diving ducks, for the most part canvasbacks and redheads, rode like a flotilla of ships on the three-foot swells along the lee shore of the Bay." The outlaws reminisced about flocks of redheads over half a mile long and nearly as wide; they recalled hunting with lights at night, stealthily moving their boats toward the "meowing" of the redheads mixed with the gutteral croaks of the cans, and firing their enormous punt guns just as a raft rose from the water in order to catch as many as possible in the gigantic pattern of shot.

Grover Cleveland, though he was one of our more portly Presidents, was a vigorous outdoorsman and an ardent waterfowler whose writings clearly reflect the conditions and the conflicting attitudes of his time. Market shooting (as well as bird trapping) was legal and, in fact, regarded as a tolerably respectable trade. Tons upon tons of ducks, geese, swans, shorebirds, and even bobolinks were shipped hither and yon across the country, and one has to wonder how many millions of these birds failed to reach any kitchen in edible condition. After a shot into a mixed flock, the valued species were assiduously picked up, but the "trash birds," whether wounded or dead, were left where they fell. Seasons and limits, where they existed, were generous beyond reason and seldom enforced. All the same, sportsmen like Cleveland had become vociferous in their advocacy of reform and restraint.

In an essay entitled "The Serene Duck Hunter," Cleveland pointedly alluded to himself and fellow sportsmen as an assemblage among whom "there is no place for envious feeling toward either the slaughtering market shooter or the insatiable dead shot." He and his peers advocated the voluntary restraint that is now, at last, being effectively revived – and of course, restraint was written into the rules at the better duck-hunting clubs.

Cleveland's political enemies derided his frivolous pursuit of fish and game – obviously unbecoming to any statesman who belonged to the opposing party – and he was accused in print of having violated Virginia game laws. In writing about his Virginia trip, he protested that "equally false and mischievous, though not involving a violation of law, was the charge that a party of which I was a member killed five hundred ducks." He went on to explain that he had been one of five gunners (one of whom "didn't know much about a shotgun"); that they hunted a total of four days, but on only one day did all five participate; and that they bagged only 125 ducks.

Today that would be appalling gluttony, mindless slaughter, and an offense punishable by heavy fines and imprisonment, but our standards don't apply. Those were the days when Cleveland and many others could report quite truthfully that skies were darkened by canvasbacks. Such abundance was perceived as a limitless resource that would forever replenish itself if market shooting didn't multiply and if a typical sportsman killed no more than a dozen or two dozen birds in a morning session.

Our wetlands had not been despoiled and drained. Nor were the ducks harvested by that era's ethical sportsmen wasted, as so many were by market gunners. What could not be consumed by family was given to friends and to the needy. A hundred or so ducks taken by five gunners in three or four days – that actually was the equivalent of today's voluntary restraint, and it should be remembered that Cleveland and his peers strongly supported rest days, as many as four no-hunting days out of seven in some locales where gunning pressure was severe.

Some of the younger hunters among us and some of the older but intractably ignorant (as well as the multitudes who cannot fathom, esthetically or philosophically, why a civilized human being hunts) are unaware that American conservation advocacy and laws, chiefly promulgated by hunters, date back to our Colonial era. A startling reminder appears on page 79 of Stephen M. Miller's *Early American Waterfowling*. It's a facsimile of a 1727 Massachusetts "Act to prevent the Destruction of Wild Fowl." Because the Colony's ducks and geese, previously very abundant, had been "affrighted and driven away" by shooting from canoes and rafts, shooting at night, and shooting "at a Distance from the Shoar upon the Flats, and Feeding Grounds," became punishable by heavy fines.

An even earlier Massachusetts law banned waterfowling from boats or camouflaged canoes, a restriction that would elicit outraged protests today. Maryland prohibited night shooting in 1730, as did North Carolina in 1777 and Virginia in 1792. New York Banned shooting from batteries (the forerunners of sinkboxes) in the 1830s – and a great many other such laws were enacted during the next half-century, long before the Federal government outlawed profligate market hunting.

Of course, It's equally true that many gunners scoffed at the laws and the conservation sermons delivered by the sporting press and the educated – also affluent – members of hunting and conservation organizations. They continued to scoff right through the Dust Bowl years of the Great Depression when waterfowl populations plummeted catastrophically – and when few among us would have condemned a scofflaw for subsistence hunting that kept his family from starving. All of this must be viewed within the context of the times.

In 1888, William Bruce Leffingwell wrote of the enormously abundant rafts of scaup:

> *...in the open Mississippi, carried along by the current, first approaching, then receding from the river bank...On, on they would float, until time and tide*

> *would bring them near the habitation of man. They would see the houses along the shores, hear the busy hum of life and activity, the buzzing and rumblings of the mills, – and away they go, flying up stream for miles, then quickly drop into the centre of the river and float down as before. These maneuvers are common in the spring...Then it is that the hunter standing near an inland pond, or secreted in some well protected blind, wonders what has become of all the ducks...At this same time the hunter in the scull-boat is helping himself to the cream of the day.*

In 1901, George Bird Grinnell pointed out that punt-gunning market shooters on the Chesapeake had, until recent years, used massive charges – as much as two pounds of shot to kill as many as a hundred ducks with a single fearsome discharge; and that before the Civil War, slave-owners who hired out their work force to other plantation owners stipulated that the slaves would not be forced to eat canvasback duck more than twice a week.

Spring shooting, ducks killed *en masse* with cannon-bored punt guns, skies darkened by flights of ducks and geese, birds so abundant that they were considered inhumane or unhealthy fare for slaves – those were the images taken for granted – and even after the Dust Bowl years, waterfowl, particularly the diving ducks, seemed to be almost as abundant as ever in many regions. In *A Book on Duck Shooting*, published in 1939, Van Campen Heilner remarked that "it was wonderful in the old days on the Chesapeake," but he also recalled a later expedition on Lake Winnepegosis in Manitoba where, he reported, "we put up thousands of canvasback ahead of the boat. They had torn the wild celery roots out of the bottom in such quantity that it had drifted along the shore in regular beds. I saw as many cans at one look at Kettle Bay as I've seen on the Susquehannah Flats at Northeast or Havre de Grace."

Elmer Crowell, the legendary Cape Cod decoy carver, worked as a market gunner and hunting guide for the wealthy until the First World War. One of his primary blinds, built in 1876 and used for thirty-two years, was a board fence about thirty yards long, brushed in front with small pine and oak limbs to blend with the background. To entice both geese and ducks, he used live decoys, tethering some of his Canadas in the water and "pinning" some on the beach. He and others recorded horrendous bags and skies aswarm with ducks and geese. After the war he devoted his full time to making decoys, not because he realized the bird populations had declined, but because market gunning had ended and he had established a profitable craft for himself. Spared from any glimpse into the future that would have appalled him, he continued to dispense gunning lore to visiting sportsmen until his death in 1952.

During our own generation, many outstanding waterfowling chroniclers have dispensed such lore in print, and their suggestions remain valid. In *To Ride the Wind*, Albert Hochbaum – accomplished author, painter, and sportsman as well as naturalist well-known for his work at the Delta Marsh Waterfowl Research Station in Manitoba – reported an interesting phenomenon that also occurs in quite a few regions far from the Delta Marsh:

> *Bluebills and Redheads came easily to Canvasback decoys, especially the small flocks. But, only two's and three's of Canvasbacks would come to a set-up of Redheads and lesser Scaup blocks. Indeed, almost any duck would come in to Canvasback decoys, if only to take a look. This would be early in the season, of course; later on, all duck became decoy-wise and great skill was required to set out properly for a decent shoot even when there were lots of ducks around.*

Other writers have provided comparably useful decoy tips such as the efficacy of "pipe-shaped" or "fish-hook" rigs, the consideration of prevailing wind direction in placing rigs so the ducks will descend within gunning range instead of sailing past with the wind at their tails, the need for a sufficiently sizable opening, or landing pocket, the use of one or two confidence decoys not only for their traditional purpose but as range markers, the cautious use of more than one species in a stool (the way I described my friend Dave doing it rather than a haphazard mixture that wouldn't fool a barnyard duck), and so on.

An example of such attention to detail, more valuable on some waters than others, is the observation that baldpates (widgeon) used to be called "poachers" or "robber ducks" in some regions because they steal scraps from diving ducks. They love wild celery but are poor divers, so they often loiter around rafts of redheads, cans, or scaup in order to scavenge uprooted bits of vegetation that rise to the surface. Hence, a few widgeon blocks slightly downcurrent from a stool of divers can add an extra touch of realism. An Oregon gunner once told me he used them as confidence decoys because widgeon are so alert and high-strung that their presence reassured passing flights of divers.

This brings me back to the definition of diving ducks, so easy for taxonomists but, as I mentioned earlier, somewhat blurred for practical waterfowlers. Technically, only cans, redheads, greater and lesser scaup, and ringnecks are included. But black ducks, which we know perfectly well are dabblers and closely related to mallards, are also closely related to the divers in terms of general habitat preference. Being more wary than mallards, they like big marshes and the edges of big waters, so it can't hurt to set a few black duck decoys in the appropriate locales. I'm tempted to class at least two "sea ducks," bufflehead and goldeneye, as divers.

Of course, the habits of all these birds can be modified by circumstances and changing conditions. Market gunners used to refer to redheads as "fool ducks," evidently because flocks tend to raft up in big gatherings at night and midday and then, for no apparent reason, "boil up" – making a great noisy commotion while rising up a few feet and settling back again. They're probably just stretching and sorting themselves out when they feel overcrowded. On small ponds, I've seen mallards and geese behave the same way when the crowding became intolerable. Redheads exhibit this habit now just as they did in the time of market gunning, but in my experience they do it only when rafted fairly far out on open water – where boiling up isn't likely to get them shot. And I haven't met any gunners in recent years who call them fool ducks.

Humans change their habits, too. Few of us would use No. 4 shot for divers these days. We need larger sizes because the pellets are steel, or an alloy we're content to call steel, and those pellets don't fly like lead. I still have some difficulty persuading myself that lead poisoning is a problem on many of the waters where the diving species congregate, but I do understand the logic of universal rather than spot regulation. Furthermore, there's no longer any doubt that good steel loads bring ducks and geese down just as efficiently as lead once a gunner adjusts his swing to them and observes short range limits.

In my own case, steel is a great help with decoying birds that are taken at moderate range because I'm slow – always have been – in sweeping the gun through and ahead of the target. Owing to steel's greater initial velocity, I don't have to do that; I merely put the bead right on the bird or only a trifle ahead of it and I bring down the duck. It's true that steel loses that initial velocity sooner than lead, requiring me to swing farther ahead of the more distant birds than I used to, but when the birds are high or way out beyond the decoys, there's more time for a long, smooth swing and I have no great trouble getting far enough ahead of the target to make the shot string and the bird collide. Even my pass-shooting at geese seems to be better with steel now that I've learned how far ahead to swing.

Fortunately for us and for the future of our waterfowl, the uproar over mandatory steel shot has at last begun to die away. From the first, it was about as meaningful as bemoaning bluebird days when no amount of griping is likely to make the ducks fly. The talk these days is about the North American Waterfowl Management Plan and voluntary restraint, and the recurrent question is whether it's all too little too late. Back in World War II, Dunkirk was an example of too little too late, but it was made to work because the alternative was unthinkable. The same could be said of Wake Island and Anzio and...

The restoration of waterfowl is a battle, too – a far different kind, thank God, but still the alternative is unthinkable. The sacrifice is trifling when one considers the future reward. I've curtailed my bag without curtailing my days on the marshes, and I can teach my son and daughter to purr and growl and wave a hat or handkerchief so they'll be prepared to coax swarms of bluebills and redheads into range long after the year 2000.

In this way, the *Grand Passage* won't be one of waterfowling passing into history, but will keep its original meaning of the grand migration – of divers and others – in their timeless, seasonal quests.

Rich Grozik has spent a large part of his career in the waterfowl conservation movement; he has spent a lot of his waking hours gunning ducks, chasing ducks, and dreaming about gunning and chasing ducks.

Rich is the author of Game Gun *and a magazine columnist who regularly adds to the wealth of his experience by seeking waterfowl – particularly dabbling ducks – in their favorite haunts. In "Distant Wings," he takes you to flooded timber, big water, and on jump-shooting expeditions to the prairies.*

CHAPTER TWO

Distant Wings

by
Richard S. Grozik

Dawn

Huddled behind a tuft of marsh grass at the edge of a backwater slough, gun across my lap, I grunted out my first awkward, adolescent hail call. The Cajun duck call echoed through the trees and I started my slide into the magic and mystery of a sport that has haunted me for more than three decades. The ducks didn't fly well that somber fall day, but my spirit soared as it still does every time I step into a marsh at dawn and feel the anticipation rise with the sun and the wind.

I've spent a lifetime trying to figure out what happened to me on that first duck hunt. I have come to realize the transformation from boy to man, from pedestrian to hunter, was more chance than choice. Lord knows what atavism lurks in the souls of men, but God's got to pity those who never experience the joys of duck hunting. Without waterfowl to greet me in the spring and beckon me to the marsh each fall, all my material dreams would become nightmares of self-indulgence.

So long as there are marshes ringed with cattails, rivers rich in bottomland, autumns filled with low-lying clouds and high-flying migrants, I'll celebrate the instincts that make me a hunter. And if I

Flooded Timber — Mallards
From The North American Wingshooting Portfolio
Countrysport Press

am left foundering in the wake of civilization's endless onslaught, I hope there are still a few undeveloped, unplowed wetlands close by that hold the promise of distant wings and strident calls. Filled by their seasonal treks up and back, I would be hollow without them.

Green-Timber Mallards

Early in my development as a waterfowler, I was befriended by a crusty old river rat who taught me the tricks and joys of hunting ducks in the woods. Up and down the river, he had the reputation of being able to coax spooky greenheads down through holes in the timber. His proficiency with a duck call would never win him any contests away from the river, but his grunting supplications were pure music to any mallard within earshot of his honey hole.

One evening, a couple of weeks before the duck opener, I stopped by his clapboard shanty down by the river. He was adjusting one of his callers. "Ah! hell, it ain't much," he said, snipping off a piece of reed, "but it'll get me through the season." He quickly assembled the battered wooden call, handed it to me, and commanded, "Now let me see what ya got!" I swelled up like a road-killed groundhog, puffed out my cheeks, and let go a screech that put a bit more twist into the shanty's warped rafters. Eyes bugged out from the blast, the veteran duck hunter quietly retrieved his call and said, "Son, it's not good to practice inside a building. Your enthusiasm is commendable, but I better do all the callin' in the woods this season," he said, working his jaws from side to side to pop his eardrums.

The next days raced past as we prepared our decoys and gear for opening day. Though disheveled in dress and lax with his housekeeping, the old man was meticulous about his hunting equipment. Each decoy was correctly painted and weighted, waders were checked for holes, and his open-bored pumpgun was carefully cleaned and oiled; he even rubbed a couple of coats of tung oil over his weather-beaten duck calls.

Duck hunting for me had always meant scudding gray clouds, driving wind, pelting sleet – weather with teeth in it. Opening morning arrived cold, cloudless, and star-filled. "Don't look so down in the mouth," my partner chirped as we loaded gear into his

pickup. "A bright sunny day will set the mallards to dancin' over the treetops. Dark rainy days usually shy ducks away from the woods. Now, let's get a move on," the old hunter barked. "We've got a long hike ahead of us once we get to the levee."

Nearly 5000 acres of flooded pinoaks, shagbark hickory, and other hardwoods sprawled northward from the levee. Just how the old man knew where we were going to end up in that tangle of trees was a mystery to me. We cinched up our waders, shouldered decoys and guns, and began our long trek down the levee. A faint lavender glow oriented me to the east and the rising sun. "Here's where we go in," my partner muttered under his breath as if to conceal our entry from other hunters and the ducks.

Thigh-deep in water, I followed the bouncing shaft of the old man's flashlight as we zig-zagged through the inky obstacle course of towering trunks and sunken logs. He seemed to move effortlessly through the maze, while I thrashed and stumbled to keep pace. "This is it," he proclaimed just as some unseen snag punctured my waders above the right knee and cold water embraced my leg. The old man was briefly sympathetic, said I wouldn't drown, and got to setting out our decoys. "Don't want to bunch'm up too close," he said. "That's what ducks do when they're scared. Got to space'm out just right, make'm look natural."

It was still pitch black and I asked him why he picked this particular spot in the woods. "Ducks come into the flooded timber for one reason only," he declared. "Acorns. No acorns, no ducks." His flashlight illuminated a dozen or so mast-laden oak trees that ringed our hole in the river bottoms. "Now find yourself a friendly tree to hug and do what I do," he instructed. The old man leaned against a tall oak, his eyes already surveying the treetops for hurried wingbeats. I found a V-trunked maple, draped my numb right leg over the crotch of the tree out of the water, and waited for the woods to wake up.

Darkness yielded to the dawn and the woods came to life. Woodpeckers tapped out their hollow greetings while a pair of tree-bound squirrels splashed acorns into the water as they fought for feeding rights. "Damn tree rats," my partner grumbled. "If my sights weren't set on ducks breasts, those two scoundrels would be our breakfast."

Farther on down the levy, some hunters jumped the gun

by five minutes and sent up a volley that thundered through the woods. Not too long after, a bunch of woodies came crying through the trees. I raised my gun, but out of the corner of my eye I caught the old man shaking his head no. "We're here for mallards – drake mallards," he said. "I'll tell you when to shoot."

With the sun came the wind, shoving puffy white clouds across an endless blue sky. The old man's raspy hail call startled me to attention. A large flock of mallards hooked in on his call and began to circle our hole in the woods. They were joined by another bunch and then another until the treetops were sprouting ducks. With his gun tucked under his calling arm and hugging his tree with the other, the old man sloshed his boot in the water to animate the decoys. As if on some secret cue, the huge flock locked its wings in unison and elevatored down through the trees. I wasn't ready for the crashing of wings and showering of debris that followed as a hundred and fifty or more birds settled in around us. In open flight mallards are the picture of grace, but they sure make one helluva racket coming through the trees. I chanced a glance at my partner. He was slowly shaking his head no, again. We were covered up with wild poultry – green heads shining, brown bodies bobbing, my heart pounding wildly in my chest.

We stood like statues as the mass of birds sensed the ruse and began drifting off deeper into the woods. Soon they were out of range and gone. Before I could ask why we didn't shoot, the old duck master said, "Son, you never, ever, want to shoot into big flocks of birds. You'll educate them and maybe kill more than you need. There'll be some smaller bunches along this morning."

He was right. Just when I had become bored with trying to identify the various species of oak trees we had wandered into, the old man's call began working its magic once again. Tawny wings flashing in the sun, a dozen or so mallards hooked onto my partner's carrousel of feeding chuckles and comeback calls. 'Round and 'round they went, tightening their circle with each pass. I hid my face under my hat and pressed closer to the tree. The old man knew *how* to call alright, but even more importantly, he knew *when*. The birds filtered in on my side of the decoys. I quickly rolled the first greenhead that came into range. It was the only bird we got. The remainder of the flock flared back through the trees, vanishing as quickly as they came.

My partner hadn't even fired. I retrieved my drake and sloshed over to show it off. "Nice shot," the old man said hefting the bird. "But if you want more than one chance at a bunch like that, let'm all settle into range. Shoot the far ducks first, then as they flare, work your way up to the close-in birds. Back to front is the way we do it in the woods," he instructed.

Still awestruck by his calling, I asked the oldtimer how he knew the birds were circling without looking up at them. He told me that if the water is calm enough, you can see the birds' reflections each time they pass. "Keeps ya from havin' to crane your neck and flashin' your face at 'em," he said.

We didn't fill our limits that morning in the woods, but the patient old waterfowler filled me with more duck lore than I've learned since. It was the first and last season we would spend together in his beloved bottomlands. An Asian war would take me away from the river. When I returned home a few years later, I learned that the old river rat had gone off to work his magic in the Great Honey Hole.

Sometimes, when I'm alone in the flooded timber hugging an oak as the birds work in, my calling sounds more and more like that of an old duck hunter I once knew, or maybe it's just a strange echo in the woods.

Big Water

Perched twenty feet above the water in what looked more like a tree house than a duck blind, I watched my host give his Reelfoot rendition of a hail call to a pair of horizon-hopping specks I assumed were ducks. I'm no stranger to "power calling," but the last time I heard such ear-splitting, lung-blasting work was at the world championships in Stuttgart, Arkansas.

The specks swung out over some tall timber on the far side of the lake and made a beeline toward our blind. My partner never let up; he blew them right into the blocks. Two shots rang out across the big water, and two plump widgeon were hung in the blind. I told my host that if I wailed at ducks like that in the flooded timber, I'd have the woods all to myself. "There are some lakes here in Tennessee," my host explained, "where modesty is no virtue. If I don't lean on these birds, I can name any number of blinds around the lake who will. If you want to shoot ducks here," he explained, "you gotta *call*."

Earlier that morning we had set out over two hundred oversized cork bodies on our corner of the 2,500-acre lake. "Big water, big decoys," my companion said, "and nothing rides like cork." The big jon boat seemed to groan with relief when we tossed the last of our big blocks into the water. Arranged in a classic fishhook pattern, with a nice pocket in front of the blind, the cork stool rode the stiffening northwest wind as naturally as the real thing.

As the hunt progressed, so did the intensity of calling around the lake. On several occasions, I chimed in with my duck call. It was a valiant effort, but could not begin to compare with the tone and range of my companion's brass-reed call. On the verge of collapsing a lung, I sat back in the blind and let my host do combat. His call was impervious to moisture – it seemed to thrive on it. Not once did it lock up or squeal. Before the morning's hunt, I saw him douse the entire call in the lake. I thought it was odd at the time, but he was just priming his wood-and-brass duck pump.

He worked ducks out of the stratosphere and away from other callers, dangling them over the blocks for easy shooting. Around mid-morning, just before a gourmet lunch of breasted duck and a full afternoon of quail hunting, my host retired his call and we climbed down to the boat with our limits of widgeon, teal, and mallard.

While we were picking up the decoys, my host admitted that calling was important, but a good spread of lifelike decoys was more than half the battle on big water. "Calling gets their attention," he said, "decoys make the difference. And if you're going to go through the effort of setting out a large spread like this, you may as well set out the best decoys money can buy. That's why I use cork-bodies." He went on to say that he prefers picking up the decoys after every hunt to keep local birds from becoming too familiar with the set-up. We grunted and tugged for nearly an hour before the last decoy was stowed. Tedious though it was, such a practice affords daily inspection of decoys, anchors, and cords.

Next morning the weather turned sour. Intermittent rain squalls dampened our spirits, and the gusting wind tore at the brush on our blind. The big lake sent whitecaps crashing against our tethered

boat, banging it loudly against its mooring posts. We watched a few decoys slip anchor and drift toward shore – not exactly the kind of day you want to be caught out on big water with heavy clothing and a flat-bottom boat. Before the storm broke, a few flights of birds had scurried about at dawn. But now, except for rain-laden clouds, the skies were empty.

There's a long-standing myth about ducks flying better in stormy weather. "Ducks don't like to be caught out in the wind and rain any more than people do," my companion said, interrupting our silent sky vigil. "They get real skitterish when the barometer drops. You can be covered up with ducks one day only to have a big thunderstorm blow them out of the country the next."

My host explained that the day before a big weather push was usually a good time to be out on the lake. Our full game bag the day before swore he was right.

We rode out the storm until it broke about mid-afternoon. Though we never raised our guns, I enjoyed that day on the big water. Over the years I have learned that if you accept the weather, its warmth and its wrath, it has a way of invigorating the spirit and satisfying the soul. Sometimes the wind, the rain, the sleet, and the snow are a duck hunter's only reward – each sunrise an adventure, each sunset a covenant of a more abundant tomorrow. A duck hunter learns to take what he can get on big water.

On The Jump

Nothing seems to last very long in the West. Whether it's rain-soaked plains whipped dry by the ceaseless wind or brimming spring potholes parched by the summer sun, the Western prairie is constantly tormented by wet and dry, hot and cold. Even waterfowl don't linger long on its reservoirs and tank ponds during fall migration. Spike-tailed sprig, cinnamon teal, and gray gadwall hurtle over the expanse, hustling anxiously to warmer, safer wetlands on the wintering grounds.

But matching wits with Western waterfowl and weather keeps a young man humble and an old man game. It's an austere environment that throws caution and tradition to the wind – always, there is the wind. No fancy calling or clever decoying here;

no choke-tube wizardry beyond full choke needed. Most ducks are taken on the pass or on the jump.

My cousin introduced me to the ways of waterfowling in Wyoming. With few trees to define depth and distance, the wide open can wear on a man. "You've got to learn to walk and crawl for your ducks on the range," my cousin drawled. "Can't road hunt 'em the way a lot of folks here shoot their goats (pronghorns) and deer each fall."

Our first morning out, two inches of snow blanketed the sprawling prairie. We drove the four-wheeler until the rutted road became a narrow, impassable cattle trail. I filled my pockets with high-brass 4's, parked the heavy autoloader over my shoulder, and followed my cousin toward the endless horizon. We hadn't walked far when the sun spooked the clouds away, melted the snow, and loaded down our boots with a knee-wrenching gumbo that clung like dough. We skirted a flattop for about half a mile and, other than a pair of golden eagles prowling the thermals, I had yet to see any signs of life.

Without a word, my cousin squatted in his tracks, signaled me to be quiet, then crab-walked and crawled off the path toward a man-made dike that dammed a deep draw. We low-crawled the last hundred yards before reaching the levee. The mud and stones were bad enough, but during my exertion and excitement, I didn't feel the cactus acupuncture treatment I was getting until after the shooting was over. As we inched toward the crest of the earthen dam, I could hear the buzzing gabble of feeding waterfowl. I was encased in mud from the long crawl and my mud-covered autoloader felt like a boat anchor. After a whispered three-count, we lurched to our feet. A swirl of teal and pintail pirouetted from the water's edge. As usual, my first shot filled some of the empty spaces around the flailing ducks. My second and third attempts put two large drake pintails on the water.

After the initial volley that morning, the elements had reduced my coddled auto to a stubborn single shot. I tinkered and pleaded with the gun for the rest of the hunt, but it refused to cycle shells from the magazine. My cousin's 12-gauge over-under functioned flawlessly, a tribute to his choice of guns and crawling ability. As it turned out that day, I probably would've had more success with a modified choke barrel. But then again, the distances seemed so vast

and with my usual foresight, I had left my choke tubes in the truck.

When we arrived back at the ranch house, we cleaned and plucked our birds, paying careful attention to pellet holes and penetration. Always a firm believer in using large shot on big ducks, I was surprised to discover my cousin's birds had been quickly killed with No. 6 shot. Only two of the birds showed lethal evidence of the 4's I was using. It's amazing how fast puddle ducks can leap off the water and rise above ill-pointed patterns. Here was proof that I had been shooting under most of the birds that morning.

Jump-shooting on the Western prairie can offer all the suspense of stalking a big game animal and requires much the same stealth. Wariness of the ducks, wind direction, and stalking strategy must all be carefully considered to put the birds in gun range. Scourged and aching, my body reminded me later that evening that being in shape helps.

In spite of, or maybe because of, its unforgiving nature, the prairies seduce the hunter's heart. Like the ducks that fly across its tortured brow each spring and fall, the prairie is a victim of change.

THE GRAND PASSAGE

With glaring sun and dismal rain, it can lift and dash a duck hunter's spirit in the span of a few short hours. Once you've stalked ducks in the West, its weathered face will haunt you for as long as you hunt.

Dusk

Much of waterfowling's allure has been its traditions, passed from father to son for generations. The guns, the decoys, the lore are no doubt anachronisms in our high-tech world. Unfortunately, the simple joy of participating in fall's harvest continues to be complicated by a morass of state and Federal regulations that are often arbitrary and ambiguous. And while the bureaucrats fiddle with the many peripheral issues affecting the resource, waterfowl habitat continues to be plundered by wanton progress and an apathetic general public.

Distant Wings

Remove the hunter from the conservation equation, and the bottom line will be no ducks for anyone to enjoy. The day we have to apologize to the government, the general public, or anyone else for being duck hunters is the day we will lose it all. I pray the dawning of that day never comes during my lifetime or my children's. If it does, dusk over a duck marsh will hold very little promise for an abundant tomorrow, and *The Grand Passage* will be the passing of a way of life into history.

Bobby George learned his dog training under the great Cotton Pershall, and even set that method down in print in his first book, Retriever Training: The Cotton Pershall Method *(Countrysport Press). Bob left a fine government career to devote himself full-time to training retrievers, particularly Labradors.*

For any of us who own and live and hunt with these dogs, Bob's words in "Retriever Tribulations," along with the experiences of a single day, will ring true – and could almost be called: "Life with Labs." They are vexing, infuriating, baffling, obstinate – and we couldn't live nor certainly wouldn't hunt without them.

CHAPTER THREE

Retriever Tribulations

by
Bobby George, Jr.

We motored down the Three-Mile Ditch on the Missouri side of the Mississippi River following another boatload of hunters, all of us part of a watery, moonlit parade.

In front, I could see the lights, now and then a boat turning down one of the slots toward the "E" blinds, then another party of hunters threading through the timber to one of the "F" blinds. I thought: Which would be the lucky letters today?

The night vibrated with voices, murmuring in the dark. The parade grew more sparse the farther down the ditch we traveled. In the darkness, you could hear the ducks splashing, jumping into the black unknown.

A slow boat ride through flooded timber in the dark makes me wonder about things I would never think about in the daylight. The darkness and the water are sensitizers and with that sensitivity comes the realization that man is not equipped to deal with the night.

Pearl the Lab, on the other hand, was right at home. She sat in front of me. She was already wet, having jumped into the ditch as we were loading out gear into the boat. She shivered and tested the breeze, edging slowly upward out of the "sit" command she was supposed to be obeying.

Back Door Woodies
Courtesy of Mr. Dick Ingram

"Sit," I said, following it up with a slap on her behind. She looked quickly back at me, not really startled, more a look of annoyance than one of subservience. She started to inch out of the command again and I just shook my head. We would be going through this all day; no sense hitting my frustration peak too early.

"Okay," I said, letting her out of the command, "Okay, go on."

She immediately scuttled over two huge bags of decoys, walked across a pair of gun cases, and tipped over a cup of coffee on the seat in front of me as she moved to the bow.

Jerel, who was running the bow light, trying his damndest to keep us off stumps and fallen timber, is the nervous type, and he already had one dog on the bow with him – his little chocolate Lab, Coke. He shouted some profanity as Pearl pushed Coke into him. But Jerel, a veteran of the duck wars and a long time retriever addict, simply stood up, giving the two dogs the bow of the boat. He knew it was just too much trouble, too early, to fight their little battles of attrition. I mean that, sure, we could win in a training session; after all we had the whips and collars, but the dogs always got even in the end. Somehow, they could always outlast us. The coffee cup, of course, belonged to Jerel. In the residual glow of the big spotlight, I could see that his teeth were clenched so tight that the enamel was starting to splinter.

About that time, Randy, sitting at the tiller, told Jerel to hold that damn light up where he could see, that we were late, that one of those dogs was going to fall in if we didn't get them back, and so on.

Jerel, who was already wound pretty tight, stripped a gear, giving Randy several alternatives about where he could go and the mode of transportation he should consider taking to get there.

"Here," he said to me. "You take the light."

Coke bounced over the decoys, spilling a box of shells into the puddled floor of the boat. She jumped between Jerel and me, licking both of us on the face in one magically quick motion. Jerel hates that.

And as I tried to stand in the boat with the light, I could hear him struggling to get to Coke in the dark. She was standing with her feet in Randy's lap and he was screaming at Jerel to get his dog under control and all Jerel really wanted to do, anyway, was throw her out and pick her up on the way back to the truck after the hunt.

"Feet up," I kept hearing him mutter, "she's going back with her feet up...back of the truck...just be able to see her feet sticking up..."

Right then, I don't believe you could call any of the three of us dog lovers. I'm not sure you could even call us retriever lovers, although we have a bunch of them. By the way, a "bunch" of retrievers is dog talk for having two dogs more than you've got kennel spaces.

In the darkness, watching the light on murky water, I thought of the beginning...Ahh, the beginning...

For me it started when I was twelve years old and my dad and I jumped a couple of mallards off a flooded sinkhole near Wooldridge, Missouri. One of the birds fell in the water and dad wound up going over his boots to pick it up. And although we talked about getting a dog to do that work, it never really came to pass. Until Pearl, the twelve-week-old black puppy, came along.

I should have known early on that I was in for trouble, but I just didn't know what I was dealing with. And, as long as I was ignorant about dog work, everything went pretty well. I did all the shooting and she did all the retrieving. I really didn't care that she was usually standing in the decoys by the time the birds hit the water. Anyway, she was just a pup.

That's what we always said, Jerel and Randy and I, until the dogs started getting gray hair in their muzzles. But I digress.

It was in the fall of 1984 that it was made clear to the three of us that retrievers must be trained and under control if they are going to be of any real value, other than ornamentation, on a duck hunt.

It was the opening weekend of Missouri's northern zone duck-hunting season. Pearl had picked up a few birds the year before when she was just eight months old, and this was to be the year she started doing the real work. I let her out of the truck that first morning and Glenn, our Truman Lake scout, jumped back and scowled.

"Who brought the damn coyote?"

His comment about Pearl's deviation from the American Kennel Club standard for Labrador retrievers set the tone for the hunt. The weather, like so many opening weekends around Truman

Reservoir in west-central Missouri, was almost balmy. After the morning mist burned off the lake, we hunted in shirtsleeves.

There weren't many mallards in at the time, so the pre-season scouting was done for teal and wood ducks. And Glenn had found them. Oh boy, had he found them. A few miles south of Clinton, just off Highway 13, he had located a stand of flooded timber that was serving as kitchen, bedroom, and lounge for several hundred woodies. In the evenings, they were coming from miles around to bed down in this little stand of trees.

And we waited for them that first evening. We made up a firing line, standing in waders, hidden in the shade of great gray-black oak trees, long drowned. The water was about waist deep, so I had Pearl sitting on a fallen tree beside me.

Just before sundown, they came, pouring in from every point of the compass, crying, whistling, side-slipping through the trees they came, parachuting in from tall places. We shot and shot and still they came. Our limits, everyone's limit, lay on the water in a matter of minutes, and the ducks kept coming. And therein was the problem.

After Pearl retrieved the first bird and I sent her back for another, the splashing caused by the ducks that were landing created serious diversions. The same thing was happening with Lindy, Randy's old meat dog, on the other end of the firing line. It was just a matter of good fortune when one of the dogs happened on a dead bird amidst all the live ones swimming around in the trees.

The final stroke, the exclamation mark to our frustration, was inked in by the darkness. We could not see the dogs, nor the dead birds. We couldn't even throw rocks at this point to help the dogs mark down birds. And I could still hear Pearl swimming and crashing through the brush. Woodies whistled and whirred at her. I estimated that we lost half the ducks we shot that evening.

I was angry and frustrated at the dogs and at myself. I felt ignorant and horribly wasteful and I vowed that night, standing knee-deep in a cocklebur patch next to the best wood duck hole on Truman Lake, that I would never shoot and lose ducks like that again. I would fix this dog somehow. I had read about retrievers that would take hand signals and voice commands to birds that they had not seen fall. By Jove, that's what we needed!

The next spring, Randy, Jerel and I started attending field trials

THE GRAND PASSAGE

and talking to professional retriever trainers. And we read books. If memory serves, it was in that year, when Randy and I were deep into the art of teaching our retrievers to "handle," that Lindy was banished forever from the house.

The first strike against her occurred one weekend when Randy was going to have a few friends over for dinner. He laid the steaks out on the kitchen cabinet and had seasoned them to a fare-thee-well and, humming to himself, he stepped outside to check the charcoal.

Enter house dog, soon-to-be-handling duck dog, Lindy. Front feet on the counter, head cocked a little to one side, she eyed the meat, checked back over her shoulder, slurped up the steaks, and marched quickly through the open door to the basement.

Enter Randy, stage left.

"Coals are great, let's cook 'em," he shouted to his wife in the next room. Then he saw the bare countertop.

"Susan! Susan! What'd you do with the meat?"

He went to the refrigerator. No, she hadn't put them in there. He went back outside scratching his head.

Eventually, they found the bones and a burping Lindy in the basement. She was exiled from the house for several weeks. But the final nail in the dog house came some months later.

Susan, an Oreo aficionado, had just returned from the grocery store. After she had put the groceries away, she had set the large economy-size package of Oreos on the kitchen table for her later attention. She went to the bedroom for just a moment to change clothes.

Enter the villain.

Padding up from the basement, Lindy went directly to the kitchen table, eyed the cookies, and without so much as a thought about the old jailhouse saw, "Don't do the crime if you can't do the time," snatched the whole package. Randy found the wrapper later that evening.

"Susan," he shouted from the basement. "I found your Oreo."

Oreo...Singular?

Grinning like a possum in a persimmon tree, he bounced up the stairs. Susan met him at the top. Gingerly, between thumb and index finger, he held what was left of the Oreo package. There was one cookie inside, soggy with dog slobber. Poor Lindy; she couldn't choke down the last piece of evidence.

That was the final straw. Lindy was sentenced to the kennel – for life.

Coke, Jerel's dog, was one of Lindy's daughters. Coke would have been the best duck dog the three of us ever had if we had killed all our birds in cornfields or the Sahara Desert. Coke was pretty sure that if God had intended for retrievers to swim, He would have given them fins.

That isn't to say that Coke wouldn't pick up ducks. She would. The only trouble was that it might take her 'til next Tuesday to find the driest route to the bird.

All of them – Lindy, Pearl, Coke – were related. And they were all what I would call "self-hunters," which means that they did it on their own. They hunted not for their masters, but for themselves. Their desire to retrieve was a lot stronger than was their desire to please.

Nevertheless, we did a lot of dog training that year. We trained in the mornings before work, during lunch hours, after work, weekends, and so on. We caught pigeons, we bought all kinds of training equipment, we played in the gun dog stakes held by nearby field trial clubs. You name it, we did it. We became dog men. Or, at least, that's what we thought.

All three of the dogs seemed to be steady as rocks by the time the dove season rolled around. Dove hunting provides the first shooting of the fall in Missouri and always provides a good warmup for both men and dogs prior to the duck season. By this time, the dogs were handling a little bit and, by golly, things were going to be different this year.

Pearl never stayed with me for one dove during that whole season. I wore out several heeling sticks on her. Randy fared only slightly better.

And Coke? I remember seeing her running full bore across a field of corn stubble after a dove that was sailing toward the far side of the field. She was dragging a ten-foot piece of ski rope and attached to the other end was Jerel's dove stool. I can remember wondering dimly if she'd hurt him.

Pearl had to be the worst, though. By the end of the season she would break for the bird when she heard the safety on my shotgun click off.

During that dove season, Randy took his wife hunting with us one day, and while they were sitting in a tree-lined fencerow, she asked him how he could tell who was shooting at what.

"You just listen," he said.

"For the shots?"

"No, for the dogs."

"What?"

"For instance, if Jerel shoots, you'll hear three shots, then 'No! No, Coke! Heel!' And if Bob shoots, you'll hear 'Pearl! No...No!' then the shots."

The treetops were becoming silhouettes against the sky when we finally reached the blind we had drawn. The next perilous moment we had to get past was the placement of decoys. Jerel and I left Randy and the two dogs in the blind. When the first decoy hit the water, Pearl did likewise.

"No! No!" Randy shouted. "Here, Pearl. Come here!" It's so embarrassing, hollering at dogs on a duck marsh. The sound travels forever and you know that there are hunters with perfectly obedient retrieving machines sitting beside them in their blinds, the dogs of which signed and numbered prints are made. The hunters sitting beside these dogs are grunting scornfully at the hapless slobs across the marsh who can't keep their half-breed mongrels at heel.

Pearl took one sniff at a decoy and headed back to the blind. If Jerel had cut the motor, I'm sure I could have heard his temples throbbing.

I took a deep breath and started wondering again. Why? Why have these dogs taken such a hold on me? I spend about half my waking hours trying to figure them out. What makes them tick? Why are some so good and some not worth feeding? Where lies the secret? Is it professional training? Is it in the genes? The brain? The heart? Generally speaking, the qualities I like best in a retriever are the qualities I like best in people.

I turned around at Jerel and smiled. Scowling, Jerel shook his head, "We're late, we're late, we've got to get these decoys out, come on, come on!"

By the middle of the morning, we had killed a few ducks, missed a few ducks, and the dogs hadn't yet driven Jerel to commit murder/mayhem/suicide. Randy was nodding down at his end of the blind, on the verge of sleep, when Jerel whispered, "Mallards."

Randy snapped to, his call automatically in his mouth. He talked to them, a small group of ten or twelve. They circled. And circled. Half the group landed in the decoys and Randy dropped his call.

"Take 'em!"

We came up gunning. We had three greenheads down and Coke and Pearl, as usual, were halfway to two of the birds before they hit the water. I got out of the blind to pick up Pearl because it looked like the last greenhead still had a little life left. I took the dead bird from Pearl and sent her for the last duck.

As soon as she got close, he dove. She circled. He popped up beyond the decoys and I tried to handle her back. Amazingly, she took my cast. She spotted the greenhead, who seemed to be gaining strength, and both headed for the far side of the cove about a hundred yards away. I moved down the bank so I could see better.

"She isn't going to catch him, Bob," Jerel said.

I scratched my chin. The duck was obviously going to make it to the standing timber. And, although Pearl didn't appear to be gaining any ground on him, she wasn't losing any either. I would give her to the timber, I thought weakly, knowing full well that there wasn't a damn thing I was going to be able to do about anyway.

"He's in the timber, Bob," Jerel said. "Better call her in."

"Uhh, yeah. Here, Pearl!"

I blew the come-in call on the whistle. She didn't even give me a glance. I blew the pea out of the whistle. No response. Randy and Jerel were silent They knew better than to say anything. First the greenhead disappeared into the timber, then Pearl.

"I guess we better get that damn boat out," Jerel said.

I walked back into the blind. "Naa, let's give her a few minutes, she might come up with him."

Jerel looked over his glasses at me.

"That duck wasn't hit too hard, Bob. He was navigatin' pretty good and there ain't no way Pearl is going to swim through that timber fast enough to catch him."

So here we were again. Dog out of control. Dog gone. Doggone dog's gone.

We waited. No one spoke. Ten minutes passed. I looked at my watch and thought that couldn't be possible. Ten minutes can be an hour when you're sitting beneath blue, duckless skies, or it can be a matter of seconds when the birds are flying and shooting time is drawing to a close. At the moment it was passing pretty rapidly and my irritation with the dog had escalated into worry. No one had spoken.

"Bob, we got to go get that dog. What if she got hung in some monofilament or an old trotline or something? We should have gotten the boat out a long time ago."

"You're right, Jerel. Let's go."

We motored across the cove to the timber. There was no way to get our eighteen-foot boat through the blowdowns and root wads. We left Randy in the blind and Jerel and I cruised up the edge, almost back to the ditch, and then we made the return trip to the blind.

No Pearl. Neither one of us spoke.

"Couldn't find her?" Randy said.

Jerel shook his head. Looking at the floor of the blind, I opened my gun to check the shells. Once again, Pearl and I had screwed up. I should have gotten the boat out right after the duck went into the timber. And what? She still wouldn't have quit on that duck and come back. We might have been a little closer, but that would have had no effect. No, like always, Pearl was on her own.

"There she is," Randy said. She had been in the water twenty minutes.

Jerel was standing up, a smile spread across his bearded face. I looked over the edge of the blind. Way down the slot, just breaking through the trees and heading our way, was one black Labrador retriever carrying one mallard drake, both still alive and kicking.

"Damn her," I huffed, clearing my throat. "You'd think with all the lickings I've given her that she'd mind better." I'm sure I couldn't hide the relief in my voice. The wind, as I recall, must have blown chaff into my eyes.

I went through the door at the back of the blind to pick her up. She was breathing like a steam engine when she hit the bank. I took the duck, she shook off and, as usual, didn't wait for me to pet her.

Pearl was like that. Hard. Affection was for lapdogs, not for her. Back into the blind she went and when I finally managed to pull myself together and follow her, she was sitting in the dog box, looking out. Waiting for somebody to put another one on the water.

Jerel finally spoke: "That was a great retrieve, Bob."

"I couldn't call her back, Jerel."

"That's not the point, now is it? You can train 'em to do a lot of things. Maybe somebody could even train her to be steady. But you can't train 'em to do what she just did."

That evening, heading back up the Three-Mile Ditch, I wondered about passion. Passion for doing something, anything, to the limit. I wondered if I had ever pursued anything – work, a hobby, anything – with *real* passion.

Pearl glanced at me from the bow of the boat. Talk to me Pearl, I thought, tell me how it feels. Teach me. But she only stared at me with those tough, dark eyes. And I understood.

You're on your own, she was saying.

Just like me.

Michael McIntosh is widely recognized as one of the world's authorities on the evolution, development, and use of the shotgun. His sense on history and the gun's place in the fabric of society has made him one of this country's most popular writers as well. His most recent books, Best Guns *and* The Big-Bore Rifle *(Countrysport Press), have proved immensely popular among those who own, use, and value fine guns.*

In "Gunning the Grand Passage," Mike takes a look at the development of the smoothbore gun from the earliest days of the flintlock up to the present, including an intelligent overview of steel shot and the controversy that divides those who love waterfowl. And he includes some interesting sidelights to the world of the old market hunters and their passage into history.

CHAPTER FOUR

Gunning the Grand Passage

by
Michael McIntosh

In the early days of the nineteenth century, Colonel Peter Hawker shot ducks and geese in the coastal saltings of southern England with a nineteen-pound flintlock that he called "Big Joe" – a single shot 5-bore built in 1814 by Joseph Manton of Oxford Street, London and fitted with a stub-twist barrel forged by William Fullerd of 57 Compton Street. Big Joe, its bore just under an inch in diameter, was meant to fire nearly five ounces of shot at a loading.

The good Colonel's favorite game gun was a mere wisp of a thing by comparison – a 19-bore Manton flintlock built in 1807. It weighed seven pounds, four ounces, and Hawker called it "Old Joe."

Such contrast still exists. Walk into a gunshop almost anywhere in the world, ask to see the inventory of bird guns, and you'll likely spend the next few hours sorting through a variety of goods in a dozen combinations of style and gauge, with almost infinite variance in weights and balances, stocks and triggers, barrels and chokes.

Ask the same counterman for a waterfowl gun, and things will be

Pit Blind
Courtesy of Meredith Long & Co.
Houston, Texas

simpler indeed. You'll still see all the various actions from break-open to autoloader, but from there on, the guns will be more alike than different. Most will be 12-gauge, with perhaps a 10-bore or two thrown in. They'll be long in the nose, light in the butt, tight at the muzzles, thickly padded with rubber at the heel, and if any of them weighs less than eight pounds, it'll be a wonder.

What unifies them all, both in fact and by implication, is a clear sense that these, more than any others, are big, powerful guns.

Wildfowl guns have always been big and powerful, once to an extent that now seems almost incomprehensible. Behemoth that it was, Big Joe was only a shoulder gun and therefore far from the biggest joe in the fowler's arsenal. Like dozens of other ardent British wildfowlers, both sportsmen and professionals, Hawker was extremely fond of punt-gunning, the business of sculling a punt-boat quietly up to a raft of birds resting on the water and raking them with enormous charges of shot from guns that literally qualified as cannon.

The typical punt gun might weigh a hundred pounds, its barrel eight or nine feet long, its bore anything from an inch and a quarter to more than two inches across. Some were even larger, fitted with barrels the size of drainpipes. Even the small ones could hold as much as two pounds of shot at a time. Peter Hawker's own pet punter, now a museum piece, is a 193-pound, side-by-side double with barrels just over eight feet long and bores an inch and a half in diameter. One side is flintlock, the other percussion – which meant that the Colonel could shatter his last flint or run out of caps and still have a single-barrel to finish out the day. With a pound of shot in either tube, such temporarily reduced firepower probably wouldn't be a severe hardship.

Hawker's gun aside, the great majority of punters had only one barrel. The earliest naturally were flintlock muzzleloaders, many of which were later converted to caplock. Improved versions, built as late as the 1880s by Holland & Holland, Greener, and others, used various types of breechloading actions.

There was similar variety among the ways of mounting the guns in the punts, from simple wooden chocks to forged-iron swivels. Recoil was always a problem, and in more than one documented instance, the big guns proved equally lethal at both ends. Hawker invented a mount fitted with stout springs to help absorb the kick.

Smaller guns often were rigged to the boats with systems of rope. Larger ones frequently were padded with gunnysacks packed with sea oats or set into wells built into the boat floors and filled with sawdust and pine needles.

In America, hunters used punt guns in Long Island Sound, on Chesapeake Bay, down the Atlantic coast to the Carolinas, and to a lesser extent on the great inland rivers. The American-made versions were not so finely built (nor, actually, so widely used) as their English counterparts, and no American breechloading punt gun has yet turned up. Even in their heyday, there probably were no more than a hundred punt guns in the whole country.

Although they digested loads that seem astronomical by current standards, the big punt guns weren't quite the angels of death and destruction that popular myth would have them be. True, a pound of shot can do terrible damage (and punters always used shot; the stories of guns loaded with nails and broken glass are hogwash), but the birds have to be rafted tightly, and the gunner has to get close without spooking them. And even at that, a pound of shot can only spread so wide and shoot so far. Thirty ducks was an average take at a single firing, and shots came few and far between.

Battery guns were more effective. These began as four or five shoulder guns fastened side by side to a plank with a wire strung through the triggers so they could all be fired at once, and soon evolved into nothing more than several barrels – either cannibalized from old muzzleloaders or, often enough, lengths of iron pipe – fixed to a heavy wooden (or in some cases, concrete) frame and ignited by a common priming charge. A typical battery might comprise as few as three barrels or as many as ten. Like the punt guns, batteries were mounted in boats and most often used to shoot wildfowl at night, aided by the soft light of a kerosene lantern set on the bow. Bores generally were small, seldom larger than 4-gauge and often as narrow as 12, but with barrels arranged in a fan-shape to broaden the field of fire, the batteries could lay out a blizzard of lead. Some gunners used two or even three batteries at once, stacked in tiers, the lower one set to fire into a resting flock and the others elevated to catch the survivors as they rose in a panic.

The punters and battery-gunners made up a minuscule portion of the wildfowlers on either side of the Atlantic, but Peter Hawker and Big Joe were decidedly in the mainstream. For every man who took

Gunning the Grand Passage

his ducks and geese by dozens at a time with boat-mounted artillery, a hundred others went afowling with shoulder arms that amounted to punt guns in miniature. Gunmakers in Britain, Europe, and the United States turned out 4, 6, and 8-bore fowlers, single-barrels and doubles, flintlocks, caplocks, and cartridge guns. They were big, long, and heavy, and they served to define a class of shotguns that we still think of, generically, as "waterfowl guns."

  In the beginning, practicality shaped the physical nature of wildfowl guns. Discounting the miniatures – the teal and their ilk – ducks are big birds, geese and swans larger still. All of them are powerfully muscled, stout-boned, thickly feathered, and easily capable of flight at altitudes well beyond the effective reach of even modern ammunition. Add in keen senses of hearing and sight, leaven with a wary nature and a fondness for habitat essentially hostile to humans, and what comes out are the most demanding game birds on earth. Consequently, waterfowl shooting by and large has always required substantial quantities of heavy shot driven by stiff powder charges, and that was the key factor in the wildfowl gun's evolution.

Black powder is relatively slow-burning stuff, and if it's to send a shot charge off at peak velocity, it has to be confined long enough for the entire powder charge to burn and release its gases. Since there obviously is no way to hold the shot in place until the powder churns up maximum thrust, the only solution is to lengthen the barrel.

According to a formula worked out by the great English gunmaker Westley Richards, the optimum length of any barrel is 40 times its bore diameter. That works out to a shade over 29 inches for 12-gauge, exactly 31 inches for 10-gauge, 33.4 inches in 8-bore, 36.76 inches for 6-bore, and a whopping 42.08 inches for the 4-gauge. Richards' dictum applied to all barrels, of course, not just those of wildfowl guns, and that's why 30-inch tubes were standard for the 12-bore gun in both the British and American trades. Writing in 1910, when smokeless powders had all but taken over the shooting scene, W.W. Greener suggests that equally good results accrue to barrels slightly shorter than the theoretic maximum, observing that 12-gauge barrels of 28 inches "seldom fail to give complete satisfaction."

He was right, but gunning tradition changes slowly, and the old standards still persist. Long barrels now contribute more to gun-handling than to ballistics, but a wildfowl gun would hardly look right without them.

As the chemical nature of black powder served to determine how long a gun barrel ought to be, the ballistic nature of shot did much to dictate bore size. Throughout the nineteenth century and into this century as well, wildfowl guns were big-bore affairs. Long shots at big, tough birds call for sizeable doses of big, heavy shot pellets, and those work best in large bores.

In a muzzleloading gun, the shooter is free to manipulate his quantities of both powder and shot virtually at will, limited only by the stresses that his gun will bear. With the advent of breechloaders, however, came standardized ammunition, and in the early days, standard loads, gauge by gauge, tended toward the light side. While the English found 3¼ or 3½ ounces of shot sufficient in a 4-gauge gun and 2½ ounces an optimum 8-bore load, the standard 10-gauge cartridge carried only 1¼ ounces.

American gunners often went lighter yet. In the 1870s, most of the wildfowlers around Chesapeake Bay, particularly the market shooters, preferred 8-gauge guns loaded with seven drams of black powder and 1¾ ounces of heavy shot. In its 1916 catalogue, Winchester offered 8-bore cartridges with 1½ and 1¾-ounce smokeless-powder loads (2-ounce loads only with black powder); you could buy 10-gauge Winchesters with 1¼ ounces of shot, but the majority had only 1⅛ ounces.

Why so little shot in such relatively large bores? Several reasons. For one, both black and early smokeless powders were brutally hard on shot. Black powder is semi-explosive and bashes shot pellets together at the moment of ignition; the early nitro powders did much the same thing. Then, because there was nothing between the shot column and the barrel, the pellets were sent scraping down the bore, wiping themselves lopsided. Once in the air, all the pellets on the outside of the column peeled off as useless "flyers," as did a fair number of the others, especially those at the rear of the column, flattened by pressure when the powder charge went off. The shorter the shot column, relative to bore size, the less stress is applied to the pellets nearest the powder and the fewer pellets get chewed up through contact with the barrel.

Long shot columns also promote "stringing," the phenomenon by which a shot charge stretches out into a lengthening cloud once in the air. Even by the end of the 1910s, typical factory cartridges produced shot strings in which trailing pellets might lag thirty feet or more behind those at the head of the swarm. Since a shot swarm contacts the target with only a portion of its cross section, having pellets strung out from hell to breakfast leaves enormous gaps in the pattern.

The American ammunition industry solved most of these problems, beginning in the '20s with John Olin's progressive-burning powders, which pushed rather than blasted pellets down the bore; followed shortly after by hard shot, which keeps its spherical shape better than pure lead; and culminating in the early 1960s with polyethylene shot-cup wads that both cushion the shot charge when the powder ignites and also form an effective buffer between the pellets and the barrel walls.

Modern powders promote far shorter shot strings than the old stuff did, but stringing is still a problem when we try to fire more

shot than a gun barrel can efficiently handle. Twelve-gauge loads crammed into 20-gauge cases unfortunately are popular among those who believe that more inevitably is better. Actually, you do get more of certain things from a hot-rock, three-inch 20-gauge shell, just as you do from a 12-gauge case the length of a flashlight – you get more shot, more stringing, more noise, more chamber pressure, more recoil, and more expense in buying the bloody things. What you *don't* get is more efficient ammunition. Modern technology is wonderful, but it can't make the proverbial silk purse from a porcine ear. A standard charge, its length in proper balance with its diameter, will do everything that any gunner needs done, provided he puts it where the target is.

A final and perhaps the most compelling reason for large-bore wildfowl guns is that big bores generally handle big shot much better than small bores do. Almost any barrel, from 28-gauge on up, will efficiently pattern shot of No. 6 or smaller, and many, but by no means all, 12-gauge barrels will do the same with No. 4. But it's a rare 12-bore and an even scarcer small-gauge that will evenly distribute a charge of No. 2 shot or larger. For those, the bigger bores are decidedly better.

Just as there is a point of diminishing returns in the relationship between bore size and the length of a shot column, so a similar effect seems to obtain in the relationship between bore size and pellet size. Small pellets snuggle comfortably together in almost any cartridge case. They settle closely bunched into relatively even layers and on the way down the bore, push against one another in lines of force fairly well parallel to the barrel. Large shot will do the same, but because of its greater diameter, it needs more space.

To illustrate the concept, fill a one-pound coffee can with marbles and another with golf balls. The marbles occupy the space efficiently, but golf balls so confined will lie at all sorts of odd angles to one another with lots of empty space between, like randomly bunched billiard balls ready to scatter in several directions as they transfer vectors of force from one to another – which essentially is what happens to big shot pellets in a small bore. If made of soft lead, they beat the hell out of each other; even if alloyed or plated, they tend to push one another off-course.

With the coffee can experiment, you can also see that simply stacking more balls into a space of the same diameter won't improve matters; you could double or triple the depth of the can, but all you'd have is a taller column of still-misaligned pellets. The larger objects require more diameter, not more depth. So, pour the golf balls into a three-pound coffee can – give them, in other words, enough room to spread out and settle in with one another – and they become the equivalent of marbles in the smaller can.

Ammunition-makers and advanced handloaders are able to mitigate the problem somewhat by buffering shot columns with ground-up polyethylene, which when properly settled, fills the spaces between pellets, cushions them from contact with one another, and helps them fly true to the course determined by the barrel. Using this approach about twenty years ago, Winchester developed a splendid line of cartridges under the trade-name Super-X Double-X – 12-gauge rounds that handle large shot at a level once the almost-exclusive property of the big-bores.

In W.W. Greener's time, such high technology belonged to a scarcely dreamed-of future. As he puts it, "The double 8-bore is recognised as the standard wild-fowling gun." It might be a fifteen-pound "Magnum" with barrels a yard long, or an eleven-pound lightweight built to fire 2½ ounces of shot from a thin brass cartridge. In either case, Greener cites its practical range as eighty to a hundred yards. Mr. G.A. Passingham, in a January 1896 letter to *The Field*, declares the 8-gauge double "handy."

The big guns were popular here, too. Eastern gunners preferred doubles, while "Westerners," prowling the teeming marshes of the lower Ohio, Illinois, and Mississippi rivers, were fond of single-shots. Fred Kimble, perhaps the most famous of the Illinois River Valley gunners and one of several people around the world who in the 1860s more or less simultaneously discovered the concept of choke boring, shot his way nearly into legend with a choked muzzleloader of about 9-gauge, built by gunmaker Joseph Tonks of Boston.

At the time, the Tonks may well have been the only choke-bored gun in all of Illinois, and Fred Kimble knew how to use it. Over seventeen days' shooting during the spring of 1872, he killed 1,365 ducks and five brant; his daily take ranged from a low of 57 birds on March 7 to a high of 128 wood ducks on March 12. At Spring Lake a few years later, he took 122 wood ducks between sunrise and nine

o'clock on a single morning.

In this country, the big-bores were most popular during the muzzleloading age, but American gunmakers turned out some 8-gauge breechloaders as well. Hunter Arms built a few L.C. Smith 8-bores between 1895 and 1898. Dan Lefever offered 8-gauge breechloaders in several versions, including his side-cocking gun of the early 1880s and his great Automatic Hammerless design, patented in 1885. Lefever Arms catalogues continued to advertise 8-gauge until 1892. Parker built them as well, both as hammer guns and hammerless, barreled in both twist and fluid steel, and they remained catalogue items as late as 1912.

Parker probably built more 8-gauges than any other American maker, but none made them in great numbers. Factory records show only about thirty such L.C. Smiths. Lefever 8-bores are about as rare as Lefever 14-gauges. Ithaca apparently built none at all, nor did A.H. Fox.

At any rate, the majority of American fowlers were by the turn of the century largely committed to small guns. Chesapeake Bay sinkbox gunners had long favored the 10-gauge anyway.

A sinkbox (sometimes called a battery box, although they never were used with the battery guns I described earlier) resembled nothing so much as a floating coffin – a shallow, man-sized box with two or three feet of wooden planking sticking out on the sides and wooden or canvas wings hinged to the front and rear. With the whole thing ballasted down to virtually no freeboard, the gunner simply lay on his back in the box, a gun at either hand, the rig surrounded by 200 to 300 decoys. The decking and the hinged wings dampened the waves well enough to keep the box from shipping water in even a fifteen-knot wind.

Its low profile is the key to the sinkbox's success. Lying motionless with his head slightly propped, the gunner could scan a wide field of view for approaching ducks. Since his field of fire was considerably more restricted, the decoys typically were arranged to toll the birds in from the front, usually at a slight angle depending upon whether the gunner was right or left-handed. At the propitious moment, he had only to raise up and take his first two shots at point-blank range, switch guns, and take two more as the ducks flared off.

Later rigs sometimes were built with deeper wells so the gunner could sit upright, and yet others were made as two-man boxes of both lay-out and sit-down design. Regardless, sinkboxes are deadly affairs. Three hundred birds falling to a single battery in a day wasn't unusual; a daily kill of 500, mostly canvasbacks and redheads, was exceptional but by no means rare, especially when combined with widespread baiting practices.

New York was the first state to ban sinkboxes, although the prohibition, enacted in 1834, was so widely ignored that it subsequently was repealed. Ohio outlawed them in 1852, New Jersey in 1879, and Michigan in 1897. Nonetheless, sinkboxes remained legal in Maryland and North Carolina until 1935.

Sinkbox shooters liked 10-bore guns because they were light enough to handle quickly but still big enough to kill at good distances. They liked long barrels, too, at least 32 inches – not because they found any ballistic advantage in them but simply because long tubes allowed the muzzles to rest on the footboard. A short-barreled gun, apt to slide down inside the box, could be hard to get quickly into action, and an errant shot, common enough with birds coming fast and a shooter's hands numbed with cold, could easily blow off the poor chap's foot. And even if it didn't, a hole in the box was a sure ticket to the bottom of the bay, helped along by nearly a ton of ballast. Drownings weren't at all uncommon.

Good as the big doubles were, sinkbox shooters presently found something even better. Beginning with Christopher Spencer's ungainly pump gun, patented in 1882, one professional wildfowler after another took up the repeater. Except for the Spencer and John Marlin's slide-action, brought out in 1898, the earliest were all John Browning designs – the Winchester lever-actions of 1887 and 1901; the Winchester Model 1893 pump and its successor, the great, rugged Model 1897; and Remington's Model 11 autoloader, probably the deadliest of them all. With the repeaters came a new age.

Aside from the lever-actions, none of the mechanical guns were built for cartridges larger than 12-gauge; but what the gunners lost by way of ballistics, they more than made up in sheer firepower. Even straight from the factory, the repeaters offered three times as many shots between loadings as a double, and market hunters were quick to install magazine extensions, some of which could hold a dozen cartridges. Using them in pairs, a good shot in a well-placed sinkbox could bring down a virtual rain of ducks.

THE GRAND PASSAGE

In December 1898, an unspecified number of hunters, each armed with two repeating guns, made a duck-shooting trip on Otay Lake in California. They rowed the length of the lake three times, jump and pass-shooting as they went, and killed 1,502 ducks in less than four hours' time. The newspaper report says that each man got a total of twelve shots before reloading his brace of guns, so they clearly were not using magazine extensions. When the story was published, California sportsmen's clubs rose up in righteous wrath and pressured the state legislature to approve a bill banning the use of repeating guns. The California Supreme Court struck down the law on grounds that it exceeded the state's jurisdiction; the state could specify bag limits if it wished, but not the type of gun used to take them.

Even though the law approved of repeating guns, a substantial population of sportsmen nationwide did not. Some of the charges leveled against the guns themselves – claims, for instance, that magazine springs would bulge cartridges to the point where they wouldn't chamber – were as nonsensical as some indictments previously brought against breechloaders, steel barrels, and nitro powder. More interesting, however, were the ethical questions. Repeating guns were branded as game destroyers and pot-hunters' tools, and those who would use them were labeled game hogs bent on wiping out every bird in sight.

It may seem curious that such sentiment should be so widely voiced in an age when shooting ducks on the water was not thought unsporting; when baiting and night-shooting and trapping were commonplace; when shorebirds and prairie chickens and passenger pigeons and waterfowl – indeed, nearly all game animals – were taken in thousands by firelighting, by nets and snares, and by virtually unregulated shooting throughout every season of the year. Curious perhaps, but from another perspective, understandable.

By the 1890s, it was obvious that American wildlife populations were in serious decline. The real culprits were a continuously expanding human population, wholesale destruction of habitat, and a thriving commercial market for wild game; but true to its historical lights, the public at large found that explanation too complex and blamed the hunter instead. The sportsman, true in turn, to his own lights, called upon himself and his comrades to exercise restraint. Likely it will ever be thus: The great mass of

humanity insensibly consuming resources on a truly awesome scale while the hunter attempts to stem the destruction by imposing ever-greater restrictions upon his own sport, all in aid of the wild world and the creatures he so dearly loves – a David in shooting clothes, willing to shrink his own keenest pleasures down to the nub in the face of an immense and ultimately unstoppable Goliath.

As it turned out nearly a hundred years ago, the breaking point came not in response to wildlife being slaughtered for the urban markets nor for habitat blithely wasted through ignorant land-use, but rather as a result of fashion in ladies' hats.

From about 1875, feathers were the decoration of choice for feminine headgear. In the first ten years or so, game bird feathers, byproducts of the wild-game markets, were largely sufficient for the demand, but by the mid-90s the millinery trade was awash in egret plumes, feathers of all species, and entire skins of everything from songbirds to hummingbirds. For those who had some grasp of both the scope and the effects of such wholesale carnage, enough finally was enough. After a massive campaign of public outrage that extended from newspaper society columns to church pulpits all across the country, Iowa Congressman John Lacey in 1899 introduced legislation to proscribe interstate shipment of wildlife, feather, and skins.

Sportsmen's clubs nationwide had for two decades gradually succeeded in establishing restrictive game laws in state after state. Now, with the Lacey Act as a foundation, they brought their influence to bear at the federal level. By 1910, a combination of public sentiment and diminishing flocks had already reduced waterfowl market hunting, but ducks and geese could still be legally bought and sold. Congress, in 1913, passed legislation that proscribed market hunting altogether, but the law was found unconstitutional. A second act, passed in 1918, prohibited the sale of waterfowl, and that one, declared constitutional by the Supreme Court in 1920, did the trick.

Among those who harbor an oversimplified view of history, it has long been fashionable to blame the market hunter for every wildlife disaster since the dinosaurs went extinct. The same sort of thinking is current still among those well-meaning people – sublimely ignorant of biology, zoogeography, and almost everything else that has to do with the reality of wildlife – who blame the sport hunter for the loss of wildlife whose habitat has been paved over, drained, polluted, plowed bare, grazed to a billiard-table nap, or simply dispossessed by superhighways, shopping malls, and glitzy condos. There's nothing admirable about killing 500 ducks a day, but given the circumstances that existed in the last century, sport hunters today have no reason to accept any hair shirt of communal guilt. There was money in market hunting, and market hunters approached it as a business, not a sport, serving a function hardly different from that of workers in a slaughterhouse. That their raw material was a product solely of nature rather than of animal husbandry is irrelevant to the fact that where there's money to be made, wildlife always has and probably always will pay the price.

Market hunting has been illegal in the United States for more than seventy years, but it still exists and exists to an astonishing scope. In his fascinating book *The Outlaw Gunner*, referred to elsewhere in this book, Harry Walsh reports that in the early 1970s an agent of the U.S. Fish & Wildlife Service estimated the annual market-hunting take at almost a half-million birds. Those birds were killed for money, not for sport, and there is little reason to suppose that any fewer die for the same reason today. Even so, it's a negligible figure compared with what's lost through habitat destruction.

Certainly, it's better that we should learn from history than simply to deplore past mistakes even as we repeat them. Sport hunters clearly know those lessons well. How intelligent we behave as a culture remains to be seen.

Sportsmen of the early 1920s found themselves in a new and in some ways better world. Wildfowl populations were only a fraction of what they had been fifty years before, but it was a fraction that seems enormous today, and with less competition from commercial gunners, sportsmen could enjoy a substantial portion of what was left.

Repeating guns had finally earned respectability among all but the crustiest of diehard traditionalists, and shooters were still discovering one of the greatest of them all in the Winchester Model 12.

The 8-gauge was gone altogether, its use for any game shooting ended by Federal legislation. Exactly why is not clear. According to one story, probably apocryphal, whoever drafted the bill asked some of his hunting cronies to name the largest gun they'd consider using for waterfowl, and they all picked 10-gauge. More likely, the 8-bore became something of a public-relations scapegoat. It was, after all, a favorite of the old-time wildfowlers, the darling of those who, like Fred Kimble, might take a hundred ducks a day, a group from which more than a few sportsmen were happy to disassociate themselves. Sportsmanship probably played a certain role as well, particularly the persistent, bizarre attitude that small-bore guns are somehow more "sporting" than big ones.

In any event, the 8-bore was gone, apparently with the tacit approval of even those who understood guns well enough to know that a good 8-gauge was a far more efficient fowling piece than most of the 12-gauges that replaced it. Since restrictive bag limits were firmly in place, they might have asked how X-number of ducks killed with a 12-gauge was any different from the same number killed with an 8, but if anyone objected at the time, he did so neither loudly nor in print.

The 10-gauge, too, was steadily losing ground, largely because improvements in ammunition had begun to enhance the 12-bore's versatility. No American maker, however, had yet fully explored the capabilities of the 12-gauge as a wildfowl gun. All of them offered

Specklebellies in the Spread
Courtesy of Meredith Long & Co.
Houston, Texas

"duck guns," of course, as the 10-gauge was generally coming to be thought of; all of them built 12-bores with 32 or 34-inch barrels, and those, too, were by virtue of barrel length alone seen as specialized fowling guns. That and three-inch chambers represented the extent to which the American trade had delved into the matter.

It wasn't for lack of interest. A number of people, gifted hobbyist and professional alike, were keenly concerned, and some principal actors began coming together in the spring of 1922.

Diminishing wildfowl populations and a high level of hunting pressure, particularly in the East, had combined to place a premium on a gun that would reliably deliver a high percentage of its shot to roughly the same place at the same time at distances useful to the fowler. It was a problem difficult enough to solve with big-bores; to accomplish the same thing with the relatively narrow 12-gauge barrel was thornier still.

John Olin and his Western Cartridge Company achieved the first real breakthrough about 1921 with a combination of newly devised progressive-burning powder and hard shot. Olin's shells, soon to appear under the trade name Super-X, dramatically shortened shot strings, tightened patterns, and thereby opened the door on potential scarcely dreamed-of before. Both Charles Askins, Sr. and E.M. Sweeley had a notion of how to make the most of what lay beyond.

Askins arguably was the most knowledgeable and influential gun writer of the time. Sweeley was a lawyer who lived in Twin Falls, Idaho, a shotgunner deeply interested in ballistics. He also was an intelligent, hard-headed experimenter determined to find some answers to the old problem of extending a shotgun's effective reach. Both men had fired a great many of Olin's experimental cartridges through various guns, some with specially bored barrels, and everyone finally concluded that a good barrel man was the key. In June 1922, Askins caught the train to Philadelphia, bound for the A.H. Fox Gun Company and Burt Becker.

Becker was by then a veteran of the American gun trade, having worked for both Parker and Remington, and probably was the best barrel man in the country. He had been in Philadelphia since about 1908, but it isn't clear whether he ever was a full-time employee at Fox. He certainly did a great deal of custom work for the company, and of the guns that John Olin had used to test his new cartridges, the best was a Fox 12-gauge that Becker had bored and regulated.

The Fox Company, much interested in the Askins-Sweeley project, assigned Becker and a small staff the task of developing a gun to realize all the potential the new ammunition had to offer. Through the summer of 1922, Becker and Askins bored and tested gun after gun, refining both the design and the manufacturing techniques. By October, the finest wildfowl gun ever built in America was ready for the trade.

They called it Super-Fox, and it was – a 12-gauge built on a frame of 10-gauge size, a gun that might weigh nearly ten pounds. Its magic lay inside the long, thick-walled barrels, where Burt Becker had worked some special wizardry.

Becker knew that the interior contours of a gun barrel are critical territory and clearly understood that the less disturbance a shot charge meets while traveling that territory, the less erratic its behavior once free of the muzzle. The first obstacle is the forcing cone, the section of bore where chamber diameter tapers down to bore diameter. A short, steep-angled cone abruptly compresses the shot charge, squeezing pellets together and pressing them out of round. So, Becker bored Super-Fox chambers in a taper, bringing them to minimum tolerance at the forward end; lengthened the forcing cones to achieve an extremely shallow angle; and carried the concept a step further by overboring the rest of the barrel. A 12-gauge Super-Fox actually has 11-gauge bores.

Overboring was nothing new even in Burt Becker's day. It's been in and out of vogue several times over the past 150 years, and like all inexact sciences, it has its share of detractors. Nonetheless, it works, as is made clear not only by the Super-Fox but by the current success of a number of barrel specialists in creating remarkably tight-shooting trap guns. And it works for essentially the same reasons that big-bore guns have always been more efficient than small ones.

Which is not to say that simply reaming some steel out of a barrel will suffice, but when combined with careful attention to chambers, forcing cones, choke cones, and other things, overboring can deliver astonishing results.

Fox advertised the Super, or HE Grade, as certain death at sixty yards. In the right hands and with the right cartridges, it probably is reliable enough even beyond. Supers were designed for Super-X ammunition and chambered to a standard $2\frac{3}{4}$ inches (instead of the $2\frac{5}{8}$ inches typical among other Foxes of that period), with three-inch chambers available upon request. Also upon request, Fox would regulate any Super for a specific load or shot size.

They were highly specialized guns, and Fox predictably didn't build very many of them, perhaps no more than about 300 12-gauges and only fifty-nine in 20-gauge. Nevertheless, the Super-Fox had a substantial impact on the American gun trade. Within a couple of years after it appeared, other makers went a-courting in the wildfowler's market.

In 1924, Ithaca simply lengthened its 10-gauge chambers from 2¾ to 2⅞ inches and called the result the Super 10. (Ithaca did a better job in 1932, with its famous Magnum 10, built for John Olin's 3½-inch, 10-bore shell.) Also in 1924, L.C. Smith brought out its Long Range Wild Fowl Gun, for the most part a standard 12-gauge Smith with three-inch chambers and a reinforced splinter between the barrels behind the forend lug. Parker in 1925 offered a 12-gauge waterfowl gun built on a No. 3 frame and fitted with 34-inch barrels chambered for three-inch cartridges.

Yet other makers followed suit to one degree or another. Sometime in the early 1930s, Remington introduced specially bored barrels for its pump guns, Model 29 and Model 31, and for the Model 11 autoloader. These barrels were overbored to .745 inches, about halfway between 12 and 11-gauge, given about forty points of choke, and stamped LONG RANGE. I'm told by those who've had some experience with them that they worked quite well.

Winchester brought out a Heavy Duck Gun version of the Model 12 in 1935 and a Model 21 Duck Gun in 1940. Both are fitted with long barrels and chambered for three-inch shells, but they're otherwise not significantly different from standard production models.

No other American maker took the pains that Fox did to create a truly long-range gun from scratch, but there was good reason for it. Wetland habitat continued to disappear apace through the 1920s, and the terrible droughts of the mid-30s brought wildfowl populations into ever steeper decline. That and the economic turmoil of the Great Depression left gunmakers disinclined to pay the added production costs for specially manufactured guns and barrels and left the majority of hunters unable to pay the even greater price for the results.

Aside from the Super-Fox, the Ithaca 10-bores, and the specially barreled Remingtons, virtually none of the American "waterfowl"

THE GRAND PASSAGE

guns built since the 1910s are inherently any better at handling heavy loads of large shot than are their upland-style counterparts. This isn't to say that you can't find the odd Parker, Smith, Winchester, or any other that will handle waterfowl loads like a champ – you just can't depend on it, regardless of advertising hype or fanciful model names. The only way to know for sure is to spend a lot of time at a patterning board, trying various cartridges until you find the shot size and load combination that your particular gun likes best; every barrel is a bit different, to some degree.

Even though the archetypical wildfowl gun of this century is a weighty 12-bore, smaller gauges once held a respectable place in the sport as well, thanks mainly to ammunition that steadily grew more efficient. Wherever shots could be taken at close range, 16 and 20-bores loaded with No. 6 shot were as deadly as bigger guns. Years ago, I used to hunt geese with an older man who used a full-choked 28-gauge autoloader and No. 6s. He never took a shot beyond twenty yards and always went for the head, correctly pointing out that a goose's head is about the same size as a mourning dove and arguing that anyone who could hit a dove...you know the rest. It takes some serious mental effort to ignore the body and wings of a Canada or even a snow goose that's practically in your lap, but he could do it. In less skillful hands, that little gun would have been a disaster, but I never saw him lose a crippled bird.

Now, of course, the days of the small-bore waterfowl gun are all but over, and some of what we've learned in the past 200 years about long-range ballistics and how to control it has become largely academic. We were working then with lead shot, and for wildfowling in this country, lead shot now is history.

The current uproar over steel shot has been a long time coming. Lead-poisoning among waterfowl certainly is nothing new, but only in the past thirty years or so has it become an important problem, thanks largely to ever-diminishing habitat, which has concentrated both the birds and the hunters into ever-smaller, ever-fewer areas, and which also has reduced bird populations to a point where we can ill afford the waste.

Lead is one of the most toxic elements in nature, and ingested lead shot poisons ducks and geese; that much is beyond dispute. What to do about it is something else again.

Several possibilities appeared early on. Plating lead shot with nickel or copper showed some promise, but the birds' powerful crops simply ground off all but the thickest plating. At least one Canadian ammunition-maker experimented with sintered shot; shot made from lead combined with iron. The thinking was to reduce the lead content and thereby the toxicity, but that didn't work, either; the stuff was hellishly expensive to produce and not very effective at reducing lead-poisoning.

Elmer Keith suggested restricting all wildfowl hunting to the use of No. 4 shot or larger, arguing that heavy pellets soon sink into the marshland mud, beyond the reach of feeding ducks. I always thought the idea had some merit, theoretically at least, but if anyone else was listening to Elmer, there's been no evidence.

For a variety of reasons both economic and practical, iron shot (which we call steel, though it really isn't) proved the handiest solution. Its primary virtues lie in being cheap and non-toxic, but it does pose some ballistic problems, and when the U.S. Fish and Wildlife Service began requiring its use in certain waterfowl areas, the meadow muffins hit the fan. Some hunters howled in protest like ruptured panthers, others screamed as loudly in support, and the majority simply were bewildered.

The situation quickly grew worse. Steel shot was both denounced and defended, in public and in print, by people who'd never fired a single round of it, while the few who really did have both significant experience with the stuff and important things to say about it – men like Bob Brister, for example – could scarcely be heard above the din. Worst of all, the whole matter got torn from the capable hands of professional biologists and game managers and became instead a political issue. In the end, it became, and to an extent still is, a point of conflict among hunters, management agencies, and other organizations who should all be pulling together in aid of wildlife and the sport of hunting instead of squabbling among themselves. All the anti-hunting activists together couldn't have planned it any better.

The wrangling may drag on *ad nauseum*, but the bottom line is that regardless of his opinions, any wildfowler who chooses to obey the law will be using steel shot throughout the foreseeable future. So what can he expect?

He can expect some important things to be different and others, equally important, to remain the same. Many of the principles that apply to lead shot also apply to steel: Big shot works most efficiently in big bores; the average factory-bored 12-gauge barrel won't pattern No. 2 or larger shot as well as No. 4; shot columns overlong to begin with will still string badly enough to be of dubious advantage.

The most important differences derive from a couple of simple physical facts. For one, iron is harder than lead, and iron pellets hold their shape better than lead ones do. Theoretically, then, steel pellets should fly straighter and pattern more densely than lead. In my experience, this generally has been true. I've tested some guns that performed wretchedly with steel shot, but they didn't like lead shot of the same size, either.

Taking this a step further, it follows that steel shot should require less choke to achieve close patterning, and that certainly has been my experience. Devotees of tight chokes are going to have to change their way of thinking if they want the best performance from steel shot. About .020-inch of constriction, essentially a modified-choke dimension, is all you need to get full-choke patterns from iron shot, assuming the barrel likes the load to begin with. Improved-cylinder is even better for shooting over decoys, and I've put as many as eight No. 4 steel pellets into the breast of a bufflehead – an area about the size of your palm – at twenty yards with a back-bored skeet gun that has no choke at all. As a rule of thumb, the less choke you use, the better off you'll be.

A second relevant fact of steel shot is that it has less mass than lead. If you think of it in rifleman's terms, steel shot has a sectional density roughly that of a roll of toilet paper. It'll kill perfectly well, but its lack of mass means that it sheds energy quickly, which in turn attenuates its effective range somewhat.

To help overcome this limitation, factory steel-shot cartridges are loaded to send the shot charge off at blistering velocities simply in order that it might still pack a reasonable punch at forty yards. Even so, iron shot makes wildfowling essentially a short-range sport, which is not necessarily a bad thing. Long-range artists of the Fred Kimble and Nash Buckingham stripe have always been the exception, not the rule. To my thinking, forty yards is about the outer limit for shooting anything, with any load. Heavy lead shot can kill consistently much farther than that, but the average gunner, myself among them, cannot.

As the latest wrinkle, at least one ammunition maker has introduced cartridges loaded with two or even three different sizes of steel shot. The theory is that the smaller pellets enhance pattern density while the larger ones provide high energy at long range. It's hardly a new idea; gunners mixed shot in muzzleloaders right from the beginning, and American patents for mixed-shot cartridges date at least to 1864. Nor is it a very good idea. For one thing, the smaller pellets lose their velocity faster than the big ones, thereby creating long shot strings with big holes in them. At long range, the effects of mixed shot are even worse; the small pellets aren't heavy enough to retain their energy, and there aren't enough big shot to provide good pattern density.

All too often, things meant to serve multiple purposes end up serving no purpose particularly well, and that decidedly is the case with mixed-shot cartridges, no matter whether they're loaded with lead or steel. If your shooting is close-in, smaller shot works fine; if you want to reach out, you need larger, heavier pellets. In either case, you'll get far better performance if all the shot in the shell is the same size.

Its lesser mass also means there are more pellets in a charge of steel shot than in a lead-shot load of the same weight. Obviously, the only way to get more pellets into a given cartridge is to stack them higher,

THE GRAND PASSAGE

and in order to make room, the polyethylene shot cups in factory steel-shot rounds don't have the same cushioning properties as those in lead loads. It doesn't affect the pellets much because they're so hard, but it does promote noticeably sharper recoil. To my thinking, that alone is an excellent argument against using steel in older guns.

Current factory loads of iron shot won't score barrels the way earlier ones did, but they'll still bulge the muzzles of guns with thin, relatively soft barrels and tight chokes. In single-barrels, the damage is likely to be wholly cosmetic; in doubles, there is some risk of ribs and fillets coming loose. You can prevent this by reaming chokes until there's no more than .020-inch constriction, which seems to be the point at which bulging stops. Older guns, however, weren't made to absorb the degree of set-back that steel shot delivers. My best advice is to shoot iron shot only in guns built specifically to handle it.

The most persistent indictment against steel shot is that it cripples ducks, that its velocity is so intense as to shoot right through a close-in bird, and so lacking at distance that it fails to penetrate deeply enough. Actually, steel shot will do both those things. You may be certain, though, that no bird shot completely through the body with a big steel pellet is likely to go far, and a bird merely fringed with lead will be just as lost as one fringed with steel. Iron shot is not as ballistically efficient as lead, but if you accommodate its inherent limitations, it works well enough.

Accommodation, in fact, may be the most important now facing American wildfowlers. The old days are gone, and no amount of complaining or wishing will bring them back. Our job is to accommodate the present, with all its realities, pleasant and otherwise. To those of us who know it well, wildfowling holds some special magic, something available only from the world of water and wind, of mud stiff with cold, of black dogs and long guns. It's a world well worth the caring for. If we can no longer participate in the same way that our grandfathers did, we still can capture the feeling and in the feeling lies the key.

Actually, we still own something of those halcyon days of the last century, when men of good conscience and intent sincerely believed that wild game was both an inexhaustible resource and the sole property of him who would take it. We own from the past a great lesson and a costly one. We know now that the Grand Passage could all too easily pass beyond every reach but that of memory. What we do with what we know will be the measure of what we are.

Bill McClure is one of Canada's best-known outdoor writers, and he's known to the American sporting public through his magazine columns and feature stories that grace the pages of the finer publications.

In "Canadian Reflections," he takes the reader on a coast-to-coast tour of that great land and talks of the magic of the wilderness, of wide and wild rivers, huge lakes, tidal flats, of ducks, geese, brant, and the methods and techniques of this waterfowler's Promised Land.

CHAPTER FIVE

Canadian Reflections

by
Bill McClure

Their solemn, serious honking high in a gusty March sky assures Canadians from coast to coast and from the 19th parallel to the arctic archipelago that the tiresome winter is coming to an end. Riding a southwest Gulf born wind, the big geese signal spring from Newfoundland to British Columbia and from Toronto to Ellesemere Island. Six months later, their excited gabble from the bright autumn blue heralds the southbound families which were raised in the Hudson Delta, Labrador, Baffin Island, the Mackenzie Delta, the Caribou Plateau, or the Queen Charlotte Islands...

Carried on the first north by northwest wind, their speeding, staggered September V's are soon followed by tens of thousands of dabbling ducks. On their tails come the divers. By mid-October the big waters of coastal Canada, the Great Lakes, the St. Lawrence, Lakes Winnipeg and Winnepegosis, Saskatchewan's Quill Lakes and the South Saskatchewan River, Alberta's Bow River, as well as millions of lakes, ponds, and creeks welcome the eager but tired and hungry migrants.

In our land of so much water, the birds are safely spread out and many pass through the country of their birth and never see a man with a gun. In the West our namesake, the Canadas, are joined by white or speckled varieties originating in the Arctic and in numbers beyond imagination.

THE GRAND PASSAGE

In 1988 I saw one group of snows landing in Manitoba's Oak Hammock that was so large, the event made the Toronto papers.

When nature, man, and luck are good to them, there are three times as many ducks and geese in Canada on Labour Day as there are Canadians. Lately, the Western ducks' fortunes have not been kind. Time will change the adverse natural conditions, but it remains to be seen if man is capable of treating our waterfowl with consideration for their simple need of suitable habitat in which to prosper. Parts of Canada outside of the prairies are having better duck times as we reach the end of the decade. Let's travel from the Atlantic to the Pacific, right across my country, from the region of the black duck to the home of the black brant.

The East

In Nova Scotia, New Brunswick, Prince Edward Island, and Newfoundland, the ubiquitous Canada goose has continued to broaden his range and increase numbers. Recently, Prince Edward Island has become a goose hunter's paradise as a new generation of birds has developed a fondness for potatoes. Favourite spud fields are rented out to shooters at a great price. In our three Atlantic Provinces, the black duck – whose fortunes we worry so much about in central Canada – has been at the very least holding his own. In some years, this favourite wildfowl of all Maritimers has even shown an increase in numbers in both Atlantic Canada and Newfoundland.

With a wildfowling tradition of over 150 years, Canada's most Eastern region is, with the exception of our most Northern areas, the least-altered portion of our settled geography. Salmon still run in hundreds of rivers in every province, and nesting or resting waterfowl continue to use the abundant, endless miles of brackish or sweet-water marshes. The Maritime Provinces produce a tremendous number of ducks and geese destined to move down the Atlantic flyway; by early autumn, the shallow inlets along the coast are dotted with birds on the move.

By mid-November, having fed well on agricultural fields or marsh plants, they head out down the Eastern Seaboard bound for the Chesapeake, the Gulf Coast, or Florida. Of course, the duck shooting is not as good as it was fifty years ago, but it is still good by any reasonable standard. There are thousands of hunters with warm remembrances of last year's shooting on Dartmouth's handy marshes or on the fabled cattails of Tantramar separating New Brunswick and Nova Scotia.

Up on the Tabusintac Lagoon in northeastern New Brunswick, a fast-vanishing tradition of the legal use of sinkboxes is retained. Developed as an effective shooting stand for the once-abundant Atlantic brant, the box floats at sea level protecting the prostrate shooter with baffle boards to keep out the sea. The gunner has his head slightly higher than his feet so he can watch the flocks turn and set to descend into his decoys. At the opportune time, he rises to a sitting position and shoots. The sinkbox is anchored in the shallow lagoon or the sand beach of a buffer island.

Only a very few guides continue this gunning tradition on the Tabusintac Lagoon, where even the legal shooting hours are at variance with the rest of New Brunswick. Now their quarry is the Canada goose and not the diminutive Atlantic brant, which once attracted guns from all over Eastern North America. Gone is the eelgrass and with it went the brant who now visit Tabusintac only on their northward spring journey. In the gunroom at Wishart's camp, turn-of-the-century entries in the shooting log recall the glory days of sinkbox brant shooting by men and women from Boston or Montreal. Old sinkboxes, cast iron brant decoys used to weight the box, and wooden brant decoys lay piled in a shed as though the old guides are reluctant to acknowledge the changes.

Decoys on the Eastern Shore of Nova Scotia may lay right where they were dropped in the grass along the rocky Atlantic Coast near "Gunning Cove." Their weathered eider colours and rusting keels tell of the cold Atlantic where they were last used by an enthusiastic, brave, and to some a foolhardy waterfowler. This South Shore shooter is willing to crouch in a gunning tub shaped like an inverted teacup and just big enough to hold him in a half-crouching position while anchored offshore. His precarious station floats with its wash boards just above the waves. Iron eider decoys are used as perimeter weights as required, and a rig of wooden decoys is set out around the tub. A companion mans a nearby tender boat to assist in retrieving downed birds and to take turn-about as a shooter. This is no place for a fine double gun, a retrieving dog, or the timid, but this most dangerous form of ducking is still favoured by many baymen willing to risk their lives in discomfort to take a few passing eider.

The duck dogs are farther down the shore at the southern tip of Nova Scotia. One of four distinctly Canadian dog breeds, the "Nova Scotia duck tolling dog" was first registered with the Canadian Kennel Club in 1945 but had been known in Yarmouth County for 100 years before. First called "little river duck dogs," the breed is part of the long waterfowling tradition in the area. Not far from the Atlantic, the forests of inland Nova Scotia are dotted with hundreds of freshwater lakes tucked among the rocks and spruce. Ducks and geese feed on the salt marshes and then fly back to inland ponds to rest and refresh themselves in seclusion in the middle of the body of water. The toller replaces all the bags of decoys used by most duck and goose hunters. From a rocky point blind, he crouches beside his master awaiting his command to action.

With bluebills, black ducks, or geese floating in sight, the dog handler throws a stick parallel to the shore and the dog springs from the blind to retrieve the stick and to prance playfully on the beach. His white-tipped plume wags continually to excite the curiosity of the flocks. He then returns to the blind without paying any attention to the now-curious wildfowl. The "tolling" is repeated over and over until the birds become so curious about the antics of the dog that they swim in close, often quacking or hissing to within twenty-five or thirty yards of the concealed hunter. Experts at the work describe situations where the birds have actually walked right up on shore, so captivated were they with the toller, coloured like a red fox and rendering such an entrancing performance. At the shot the toller, who in addition to being an enticer is an excellent water retriever, is sent out to fetch.

Nineteenth-century sporting books suggest that tolling with a dog was once a common pastime of many Eastern Seaboard hunters, but the practice is now limited. There are very few locales where one finds the combination of freshwater lakes, salt marshes, and tranquility necessary for satisfactory tolling. The duck tub and the sinkbox have been retained in the Maritimes and so has the Nova Scotia duck tolling retriever, a dog unique to the sport, to Canada, and to our continent.

Ontario and Quebec

It may come as a surprise, but Ontario and Quebec, our two most populous provinces, have a lot of very good duck and goose hunting within their enormous geography. Spanning from the U.S. border to the arctic and containing Canada's largest cities, Toronto and Montreal, Ontario and Quebec are home to some of the most popular staging areas for migratory birds on the flyway.

The La Prairie Basin, situated between the island of Montreal and the St. Lawrence River south-shore city of La Prairie, is virtually within sight of Mount Royal. In old days, it was a favourite duck sanctuary and remains so today. Downstream on the St. Lawrence, the mile-wide river welcomes the entire population of greater snow geese at Cap Tourmente, a Federal Management Area with organized permit shooting. Nearby, on the Ile-aux-Grues, enterprising locals guide goose-hunting parties on the quicksand-like mud flats to await the ear-shattering cacophony of 10,000 geese lifting as one off the river. It is believed that some greater snows fly non-stop the 2000 miles from their breeding ground on Bylot Island in the Arctic to Cap

Canada Honkers
Courtesy of Meredith Long & Co.
Houston, Texas

Tourmente. On the right day with favourable wind, tide, and lady luck, a limit of white geese comes easily to a patient marksman. By early November the white flocks are off for coastal North Carolina.

Farther downstream where the St. Lawrence turns salty and Quebec borders Labrador, the big red-legged blacks, scoters, and eiders are hunted by hardy Quebecers willing to challenge waterfowling conditions that on the now-vast river off Gaspesie rival those on Nova Scotia's Eastern Shore. To the west of Montreal near Quebec's border with Ontario, Lake St. Francis – a broadening of the great St. Lawrence – provides a generous haven for huge flocks of migrating birds. Scaup, en route from northern Manitoba or Ontario to central Florida, are drawn to this widening. For generations, Quebec and Ontario hunters have enjoyed layout boat and shore blind sport on these gunning grounds. When the late October northwest winds ruffle the bays, the scaup and whistlers fly from their sanctuary in the middle of the lake eager for the company promised by three dozen wooden blocks inviting visitors.

From Kingston, Ontario, where the river leaves Lake Ontario and downriver to its melding with the sea below Quebec City, the impressive St. Lawrence still affords some of our best and least-publicized duck shooting. The birds come late, cold, and unpredictably, but when they are on the move, there is royal sport. From Wolfe Island's renowned bluebill stands, or Morrisburg's great goose hunts down past Cornwall's puddle duck blinds then downstream to Quebec, the St. Lawrence is home to many spirited shooters. Best in the mid to late season, it is no place for the soft or anyone who is badly equipped with gear or judgement.

Nor is eastern Lake Ontario in December, where the determined and their Chesapeake dogs confront the ice, rock, and steely grey water tipped with white and shrouded in "sea smoke" from a bitter night. The pursuit of equally determined whistlers is work only for the committed but as thrilling as any facet of our sport one can imagine. Above all you are alone. When shooting from a tiny limestone island out in the unforgiving lake, your two whistlers taken over the grey-green December water are memorable. I would rather gun under such conditions than take a limit in a popular marsh where I never feel like I am part of anything except a crowd of shooters.

Ducks and geese live and travel in grand parts of Canada's vast topography, and whenever possible the birds select places without

people. Me too. I want to be alone with the birds in a place where, like my compatriots in Nova Scotia or eastern Quebec, I can be solitary with a minimum of fuss. Then I will not only see the birds but hear their sounds and those of the serene forest pond.

North of the big lake, the Laurentian Shield, with its pine, spruce, rock, and beaver ponds, provides a miniature duck factory too-little acknowledged for its important contributions to North American populations. Here, a hen black, mallard, ringneck, woodie, or teal may nest and rear her brood in total seclusion until the first September 20th light when the shooting starts. Until recently, access to many ponds was on foot, often without benefit of a path, as eager hunters traversed beaver dams, scrambled up granite outcrops, breathing the wonderful odours of the Northern forest in autumn. Canoes were portaged or skidded in in the winter and left hidden for opening day. Now, the lumbering and three-wheeler traffic has opened up much to the lazy with the loss of some peace for the ducks and silence for the waiting gunner.

It is here among the hard stone supporting the fragrant oak, maple, hemlock, spruce, pine, birch, ash, and cedar forests that the birds and I feel most at home.

We first met among the rocks when I, as a young man, chose to live in the Shield where after town work I could be out until dark. Intending to lure the returning into a rig of a few dark decoys set in a tiny bay on a black spruce-rimmed pond, I was often quite late returning home. My young bride was reassured by the hamlet elders at Robertson's store that "if he had matches he will be fine and we will go for him in the morning." I not only had matches but a pair of ducks the colour of the dark water they sought on which to rest for the night.

Then as now, the jewel-like waters flecked with red rocks guide the gunner as he paddles carefully out in the dark night, interrupting the beavers as they haul their logs or patch the dams which we breached on the way up to the shooting stand. Lucky is the man who paddles back out in the illuminated dark of the full moon. If you are early you must wait in company with the muskrats, marsh birds, and crows. The ducks come later, much later. The first arrivals are on duty about sunset, dripping swiftly from treetop to eye level and then down into the black water of the marsh. There is no hesitation. And on they come.

In a few minutes their passage is continuous amidst quacking, squealing, and splashing of those already down. Feet reach out, wings cup backward into reverse as the big ducks reduce air speed. The little ones come faster, and in their headlong flight they must turn sharply and bank in to get slowed down in time to land. Shooting does not slow their arrival and, remarkably, disturbs those on the water very little; they are home and a little ruckus is to be expected. Soon it is pitch dark. Then the beavers take up their work.

There are thousands upon thousands of such beaver-built shooting grounds in Eastern Canada, from tiny five-acre floods to mile-long hydraulic masterpieces with four or five control dams. The "engineers" are always alert to new projects, seemingly delighted to pack the mud and poplar sticks across any rivulet that shows potential. The ducks of northern Ontario, Quebec, and the Maritimes are the benefactors of the beaver's night-long devotion to water control. Some of my finest duck shooting moments have been on such ponds up on the Shield, but I am a sucker for tranquility. So are the ducks.

But Ontario is much more than the Shield country. Connecting Ottawa with Kingston, the Rideau Waterways, a series of linked rivers, lakes, and canals still convey wildfowl down to Prince Edward County's Hay Bay and vicinity. The myriad bays and marshes of Prince Edward jutting far out into Lake Ontario were an important historical staging area for ducks, and to this day serious hunters are able to enjoy decent sport. Not so, regrettably, at the western end of the lake in Hamilton Harbour where industrialization has ruined what was once one of our primary gunning grounds.

Over the Niagara escarpment, the famous Long Point Club on Lake Erie protects for their members some excellent ducking as do a number of smaller private clubs on the Erie shore. Several locations operated by the Ontario government provide blinds by reservation for public hunting.

Sadly, agricultural efficiency, pleasure boating, industrial pollution, population growth, and acts of God have also deprived Canadians of much of the grand duck grounds of southwestern Ontario. Walpole Island on Lake St. Clair, much of which in Indian treaty land, remains as a faint reminder of the glory days when tens of thousands of wetland acres were home to dozens of shooting camps, decoy carvers, and market hunters. All of this is gone – forever.

The Prairies

Canada produces about 80% of all the ducks and geese in North America, but the critical pothole areas of the south-central Canadian prairie alone contributes 50% of the total. Manitoba, Saskatchewan, and Alberta are the places to go if you like to see waterfowl on the move. The massing begins in late August, just when the grain is being cut, and builds to a crescendo in late September to mid-October. There are canvasbacks and redheads, mallards, teal, scaup, shovelers, gadwall, wigeon, Canadas, whitefronts, snows, blues, and other species winging over the rolling wheat fields, sloughs, lakes, and ponds. It is here The Grand Passage really begins.

You can enjoy field shoots from hedgerows taking passing shots at high flyers, pit shoots at decoying birds, or shore-blind shots at decoying cans or redheads. Or if you're lucky, you may just be able to set up on a likely dike and pass-shoot until your heart is full at birds moving from feed to water or vice-versa. I once sat in a November

prairie goose blind, removed the shells from my gun, and watched and listened to thousands of birds feeding a few hundred yards from me. As if on signal, they rose in waves to return to the South Saskatchewan at 11:00 am. The noise of their wings, their vocalizations, and the rush of wind were unforgettable. The undulating flocks vanished from hearing long before they vanished from sight across the broad, steep-sloped prairie coulee leading down to the distant river. I identified three species of geese and four of ducks in the exodus. They returned the next morning. So did I. So should you.

To enjoy prairie birds in their landscape of stubble, fallow, and sky broken only by great rivers, lakes, or small sloughs, go early or late to have the most fun. During the first week of the season, go north and meet those arriving from farther up the long map of Manitoba, Saskatchewan, or Alberta. Down from the Peace, Le Pas, or La Ronge, a thousand miles or more they wing over water and forest to the lakes and sloughs of the agricultural and ranch areas where the forest meets the grain. Then you have them pretty much to yourself. Hunting them isn't easy. You will have to scout fields, talk to ranch owners, and build good blinds at the forest edge. Be patient; they will come, right over the tops of the golden aspen, talking incessantly as if to exclude the group of sandhill cranes following them. Mostly juveniles, they will be fooled that first time they decoy. But not so easily the next, or the next. Shotguns and natural selection are the enemies of naiveté. If you choose November in the stubble, there will not be as many geese, maybe just 50,000 instead of 150,000 coming off the frozen-edged river.

Most sloughs will be ice-covered, but the endless grainfields still provide sufficient food, and the geese stay on as long as they can obtain food and fresh water. Enormous flocks of mallards do, too, and they are wary, experienced birds, moving in purposeful flight across the grey sky. They are not easy to hunt and like the geese, these late migrants are chunky birds in full feather insulation against the cold. This is the time for the giant Canadas, the twelve-pounders who thump as though they are going to split open when they strike the ice from fifty yards up. A trophy taken on his terms, on a tan, white, and black-brown landscape awaiting the winter snow cover. In a day, a week, or ten days they will depart for the wintering areas of Texas or Tennessee, Minnesota, Missouri, or Oklahoma. With them go the last of the fat fall mallards.

For four bitter-cold months, the Canadian prairie awaits the return of the first March flocks. The melting snow fills the thawing sloughs while spring rains will keep water levels high enough to welcome the ducklings hatched in the protective brush surrounding the pond. A little farther north, the teal, gadwall, wigeon, buffelhead, goldeneye, scaup, or ringnecks nest in the parkland or farther north in the Yukon or Northwest Territories. The white, speckled, and some of the Canada geese must return to their homeland early as they are bound in some cases to the arctic islands or the tundra coast of Hudson's Bay. Those spring migrants are in a hurry and need precise timing and good fortune to arrive at an opportune time for nesting. A spring snowstorm after a goose has set her eggs can be devastating. The birds have a narrow margin of error so that they can hatch and rear their families before the decreasing August daylight tells them it's time to depart for the prairie grain. This is life at the top of the continent. It is not as harsh for waterfowl using British Columbia's Pacific flyway.

The West

For mainland or island dwellers of British Columbia, the waterfowl that has attracted the greatest historical interest is the black brant. Traditionally, a coterie of devoted hunters has haunted the brant bays of the Pacific Coast in pursuit of this temperamental bird.

On the lower mainland of British Columbia, such a group continues the practice of late winter black brant shooting. The little goose, no bigger than a mallard, is always a challenging quarry preferring, like his Atlantic brethren, to fly far offshore in the autumn. It is during those movements northward when the beautiful black and white birds are likely to use the bays of coastal B.C. or Vancouver Island. They are finicky about what they eat and determined to get to where they are going in spite of hell, high water, or high winds. British Columbians who go brant shooting in Boundary Bay below the city of Vancouver are a committed lot. Their monitoring of the tide tables, wind, and movement of the flocks is careful, and it is said that becoming a brant hunter is comparable to joining a special club – a club that believes that the

handsome little crown prince deserves the best in decoys, attention to detail, and of men. The gunners of Boundary Bay have a great deal in common with the eider hunters of Quebec or Nova Scotia's South Shore. Many would be incredulous about why they bother.

One of the most pleasant memories for me in British Columbia was the sight and sound of a flock of Canada geese with wings set to land in a blue September pond reflecting the snow-capped Rocky Mountains. Many, many geese traverse the length of Canada's most Western province in their journey from north to south. Mallards, scaup, teal, and others also use the mountain valleys as migration routes.

The coastal and island bays and marshes of British Columbia provide very attractive Pacific flyway staging grounds for our birds. Duck or goose shooting in British Columbia is not as accessible as it is in other ocean provinces, and many B.C. waterfowlers make the trip across the Rockies to enjoy the prairie shooting. But so do gunners from Ontario, Quebec, and the Maritimes. A shooting trip on the prairies, well-planned and properly guided, is an experience never to be forgotten. But that does not mean that you will shoot your limit every time.

Canadian Reflections

In spite of dozens of species using British Columbia's Coastal flyway, the hundreds of thousands of prairie ducks and geese, the enormous flocks of divers on the St. Lawrence, and the bountiful numbers of puddle ducks of the Maritimes, I have come back many times empty-handed – but never empty-minded. Like many Canadians, I have seen a black duck leap from a muskeg pond on Newfoundland's Great Northern Peninsula and a red-breasted merganser family cavort with a loon family on a Labrador lake. To see the greater snows fill the sky and the eye at the Cap Tourmente or a flight of wood ducks move like jet trainers over the balsam tops of a Laurentian Shield beaver flood is to be a Canadian waterfowler. The rafts of canvasbacks on the upper Niagara were part of my boyhood, as the indescribable multitudes of the prairie landscape are part of my manhood. I need the Canada geese of the Kootenay framed by the majestic Rockies.

In a Canadian spring, we all look skyward when we hear their voices or turn to the sound of their flashing wings in an April sky. In autumn, many of us sit quietly, concealed, talking to them until we can hear clearly the wind in their wings and see distinctly the bright colours of their feathers. Waterfowl are important to Canadians, so it is with mixed emotions that we rise with respect and pride and guns in hand to do that which we have come to do.

Stuart Williams has spent more time hunting waterfowl in foreign lands than most of us can imagine. He has taken hundreds of "trips of a lifetime" (nineteen times to Argentina, for example).

And even though many of these places carry the promise of a potentially heavy bag, their greatest lure is the exotic, the unknown, experience. Always on the forefront of shooters to newly opened locales, Stuart has even visited and hunted in the Soviet Union.

And the species are as exotic as the surroundings: graylag geese, rosy-billed pochards, Magellan geese, and tree ducks. Or the methods are exotic, such as shooting flighted mallards in the shadows of ancient Danish castles.

In "Waterfowling Abroad: The International Experience," Stuart explores these fabled lands and others, and makes our feet itch to join him.

CHAPTER SIX

Waterfowling Abroad: The International Experience

by
Stuart Williams

"I cannot rest from travel."
Alfred, Lord Tennyson, *Ulysses*

Duck hunting in North America is an enlightened form of madness. One rises at insane hours, stumbles into his clothing, and, fortified with large doses of caffeine, travels long distances in the dark to make himself miserable. He fumbles with wet decoys in the darkness; staggers around in mud and icy, chest-deep waters; suffers knife-edged winds and rains; and handicaps himself with steel shot – all in the hopes of shooting a few ducks. Sometimes he will come home with none. What's more, he will have to pay dearly for the privilege.

Anyone who has long suffered the penitential rigors of North American waterfowling and who just once enjoys the gentlemanly ease and the balmy weather and the heavy bags of a duck shoot on the Nile Valley of Egypt or the Pacific Coastal lagoons of Mexico or the rice plantations of Uruguay or a goose shoot on the plains of Patagonia or among the ruins of Upper Egypt will surely conclude that perhaps there are better ways of doing things.

Just as waterfowling in the United States in many areas is in decline, so waterfowling in other parts of the world is just beginning to open up: "Though much is taken, much abides."

In recent years, Argentina has begun to lay claim to the honor of being the world's greatest waterfowling land, and its neighbor Uruguay, although without geese, offers duck shooting that is virtually as good as Argentina's. New areas in China and Mongolia will probably soon be opening, and I expect that some of the lakes in the high Himalayan valleys of Pakistan, which potentially offer some of the finest duck shooting available anywhere, will be open to foreign shooters in a year or two.

Finally, and most important, is the Soviet Union. In a desperate quest for hard currency, the Soviet Union is rapidly opening up vast expanses of hunting land that had been off-limits to foreigners since Czarist days. The Soviet Union has the potential to become far and away the greatest waterfowling land of them all. It has more freshwater surface than any other nation, vast grain–growing areas, and huge territories that are completely uninhabited.

Admittedly, one can and will routinely shoot more ducks or geese in any of those locales than he will ever shoot in the United States. Even though shooting is the heart of the matter in waterfowling, it is not the entire matter. There is a whole penumbra of ancillary pleasures that make an overseas waterfowl experience very different from a North American shoot.

I have made the long pilgrimage to Argentina nineteen times, and I hope to make it at least as many more. For me, Argentina is the greatest waterfowling land of them all. In March – early fall in Argentina – great constellations of Magellan geese arise from their nesting grounds in Tierra del Fuego and travel north. Their numbers are so vast that they shroud the harsh, wind-swept

Waterfowling Abroad: The International Experience

plains of Patagonia in shadow as they go.

Following the Andean spine of the continent, they pass Ushuaia and Perito Moreno and Las Antiguas and continue north to Esquel and Bariloche. There part of them turn eastward and stream down the long Río Negro Valley. As they go they sing the ancient song of the pampas: "*Kakk–ka–ka–kaaaak! Kakk–ka–ka–kaaaak!*" Some of them stop to spend the winter near Choele Choel, while others continue on to Conesa, and yet others go all the way to the Atlantic Ocean at Viedma. Many continue north from Bariloche to the sere, brown hills and valleys around San Martín de los Andes and Junín de los Andes.

It is in these wintering grounds that the far-traveled gunners, having made the long journey from the opposite end of the earth, await to keep their annual rendezvous with the grand birds.

All goose shooting in Argentina is done over decoys that are a mixture of silhouettes and windsocks painted to simulate the Magellan geese, the most abundant species. As geese are shot, they are propped up with sticks to enlarge the spread. Experience has proven that dead geese are far more deadly – no pun intended – decoys than the imitations.

The Magellan goose weighs nine pounds at maturity. The male is all white except for brown and gray bars on the wings, and the female is a drab brownish-gray all over. Both sexes have black bills. Because of the white plumage of the males, a flock of Magellans can be seen a mile away by keen eyes. In the flush of first sunlight, the breasts of the males – whiter than polished ivory – glow with a fiery incandescence. As the sun rises higher and the light becomes more golden, the breasts of the incoming males shine like the shields of advancing warriors. It is a sight that I have seen a thousand times, and yet it never fails to mesmerize me.

Magellan geese tend to congregate in flocks of thirty to one hundred or more. When such a large flock comes in to decoy, it comes in on a straight line and without hesitation. Because of the large number of birds, they simply inundate the shooters. All over and around them great birds are frantically beating their wings and fighting for altitude after the first shot. When they have departed, a cloud of gunsmoke wafts away downwind and small feathers float softly to earth.

After the morning's shooting is finished – and virtually all the action happens in the morning – shooters and guides and pick-up boys retire to a nearby field for an *asado*, or field luncheon. The pick–up boys and guides busy themselves with erecting a folding table, setting up chairs, and building a fire among towering Lombardy poplar and eucalyptus trees. When the fire is burning well, they bring out liters of the robust, fruity red wines from the high hills of Mendoza, and load the tables with plates of *aperitivos* – cubes of Edam and Stilton cheeses, and slices of smoked breast of goose and smoked ham of red stag. Soon huge slabs of steak and thick links of beef sausage are grilling over coals, and irresistible aromas are filling the air.

Then shooters and guides and helpers get their greedy grubhooks to work on the steaks and sausages, and all conversation ceases while they do their voracious business. Afterwards, sated by the heavy food and mellowed by the wines, they stretch out on the ground and take a long siesta in the sunshine.

The scene changes to northeastern Argentina, specifically, the province of Corrientes. This is a vast alluvial plain, watered by abundant rainfall and drained by the mighty Paraná River – broader than the Mississippi – and its countless tributaries. This is rice-growing country, where some rice-growing plantations extend to 50,000 acres and more.

It is also duck country. Ducks swarm in such pestilential congregations that the rice growers – out of sheer self-defense – poison them. Local people tell me of seeing bulldozers push tons of dead ducks into ditches and cover them over. I find their accounts entirely credible.

There is a limited variety of ducks in this part of Argentina. Most numerous are the tree ducks – white-faced and black-bellied and fulvous – even though there are few trees. Then there are the silver teal and ring-neck teal and Brazilian teal. There are also some brown pintails, and in recent years for the first time, Bahamas pintails. Most important of all of them for the shooter is the rosy-billed pochard.

The rosy-billed pochard is, for my money, the equal of the mallard for sport and for the table. It is as big as a mallard, it flies high and it flies fast, it is hard to hit and harder to kill. It must be centered with a heavy charge of hard No. 4's to bring it down cleanly. It has just one weakness: It is a sucker for a deceptively arranged spread of realistic decoys put out on one of the potholes where it loves to loaf and dally all day. Such potholes can easily be recognized by their abundant crops of duck potato and wild celery.

Seen from a distance, the rosy-billed pochard appears to be a big black duck with a white speculum and white pinfeathers. Shoot one, however, and you will see that the rosy-bill is a bird of most magnificent plumage. The chest and neck have a beautiful purple-green iridescence. The most striking feature of the male rosy-bill is its pink beak and a fiery red bulbous knob, just where the beak joins the head. Seen in the first sunlight of the morning, the beaks of an approaching flock of rosy-bills glow like coals.

All duck shooting in this part of Argentina is done over decoys. In the morning and the evenings, the gunners gather on the potholes and the paddies. They shoot, loading and firing nearly as fast as their fingers will fly; in their dreams later that night, the skies are filled with ducks from horizon to horizon. They shoot and shoot and shoot all night, and never miss a bird.

To hunt waterfowl in Argentina means living in forlorn towns far out on the plains of Patagonia; it means riding across those plains

Teal & Tree Ducks
Courtesy of Mr. and Mrs. Earl Burke

Waterfowling Abroad: The International Experience

while listening to tango songs of faithless loves and violent death; it means *gauchos* moving great herds of cattle across those plains; and it means sitting down at mealtime to large spreads of succulent grass-fed *bife de chorizo* or *bife de lomo* or *bife especial*, with side dishes of *gnocchi* or *ravioli al sugo* or *tagliatelle alla carbonara*. It means the realization that you can shoot a lot better than you thought before you made your first visit there. Finally, it means the realization that you are one of the fortunate few to have enjoyed the world's greatest waterfowling.

Denmark is an altogether different experience. Argentina is a vast, raw, frontier country; Denmark is small and sophisticated and gracious. All waterfowling in Argentina is for purely wild birds; in Denmark it is primarily for incubated and keepered birds. The comparison is certainly not meant to belittle the quality of Danish ducking sport, however. It is the best mallard shooting in the world.

Gamekeepers incubate large numbers of mallard eggs in the spring and rear the ducklings in progressively larger pens. At an appropriate time the birds are released. They never go very far away, because they are so heavily fed on the estate where they are raised. These ducks often have the effect of shortstopping some wild mallards heading south in the late summer or early fall. Those wild mallards enjoy the big feeds put out for the local ducks, and usually go no farther south.

The shooting begins in late August. A group of six to eight guns surrounds a small lake, and a veritable armada of boats with dogs is sent in to rouse the ducks off the water. They get up by the hundreds – sometimes thousands – in an unforgettable surge. They inevitably fly over the strategically placed shooters. The shooting begins in earnest, and the shooters' skills are sorely tested. Within fifteen or twenty minutes the ducks have all departed and a calm ensues. However, they have such an attachment to that lake that soon they attempt to return. They come in, twisting and sideslipping and rolling and darting through the branches of ancient oak and beech trees. If there is a wind, they fly as evasively as bats. It is under such circumstances that Danish duck shooting excels. Even though most of the birds are keepered, nobody who has ever shot them under such circumstances will say that they are easy. In fact, they are as difficult and sporting as any duck that flies.

Because each estate is usually shot only one day a year, and the number of shooters is limited to eight, there are no bag limits. In fact, shooters are encouraged to shoot as many ducks as possible, because all the ducks are sold to gourmet restaurants in Copenhagen at seven to eight dollars each. A bag of 400 to 600 ducks per day is common. Missing is a social *faux pas* that is seriously frowned upon. Each duck missed is like eight dollars flying away forever, for the birds are a cash crop there, like the driven pheasant of England.

As wonderful as the shooting is, it is only half the pleasure of a Danish estate duck shoot. Shooters stay in castles and gracious manor homes where they mingle with counts and dukes and barons and their ladies. Lunches and dinners are grand gastronomical ceremonies. Typically, shooters sit down to lunch at long banquet tables. They start out by drinking many a "Skol!" with glasses of Acquavit so potent that it turns your mouth into a blowtorch and so cold – it doesn't freeze until it's –60 degrees Fahrenheit – that you have to be careful, lest you freeze your lips and tongue solid. Next follow smoked herring and pickled herring and herring marinated in eight different sauces. Then come smoked salmon and smoked sea trout.

For the main course there might be turbot or lobster or prime rib of beef. As each course is taken away you think that surely that one must be the last. You are wrong. In the meantime under the table, massive Labs and Chesapeake retrievers – which have fetched ducks all morning – are persistently pushing on your legs, demanding a handout. Surreptitiously you pass under the table a beef bone or a baked potato or a piece of buttered bread. You think that this must – like missing – be a serious breach of etiquette, until you hear the cracking of beef bones and bread crusts under the entire length of the table. It all ends with the contented thumping of tails on the floor while everyone downs a final Carlsberg or Tuborg.

At the end of the day all the ducks are laid out in arrow-straight lines, drakes up front and hens behind. Then a horn signal calls all

THE GRAND PASSAGE

the shooters to attention. The total of the day's kill is announced, and then further horn signals are played while shooters continue to stand at attention to pay their last respects to the fallen birds.

Duck shooting in Czechoslovakia is rather similar to that in Denmark. It is some of the finest mallard shooting anywhere, and the circumstances that permit that excellent shooting have been created almost entirely by human intervention. During the Middle Ages, southern Bohemia – the part of Czechoslovakia where all the duck shooting is concentrated – was a vast morass where malaria and poverty ruled supreme. Ambitious Dominican friars set about draining those swamps to create arable land. Over several centuries, they created an extensive network of thousands of ponds with interconnecting canals and locks. The peasants planted corn and wheat and oats and barley on the newly drained land. Water weeds grew up along the banks of the ponds and canals. Carp were intensively farmed in those ponds. Soon, great swarms of migrating ducks began to pause here on their southward journey, and each year they stayed longer and longer.

The usual *modus operandi* of duck shooting in Czechoslovakia is to surround a large pond or small lake with six to ten shooters and then send in two or three boats with shooters and Drahthaars, the preferred dog. Then the action proceeds much as in Denmark. On a good day fifteen or twenty years ago, such a group might shoot 300 to 350 mallards a day. Today, however, thanks to pesticides and the extensive clearing of water weeds, a bag of 150 ducks a day would be considered good.

What the Czech duck shooters have lost in numbers of ducks they have compensated for in conviviality. After each shoot there is a social gathering outdoors or in a local inn or restaurant. If it takes place outdoors, hunters grill sausages over an open fire and wash them down with copious draughts of Pilsner Urquell, the best beer in the world. Many a *na zdravi* is toasted with vodka, and the King of the Hunt – the high gun for the day – is announced and applauded. The head gamekeeper will make a brief speech commending the safe gun handling and the shooting skills of the hunters. All the hunters will, of course, be attired in the loden green clothing that is traditional – if not obligatory – for hunters in the Germanic countries and their neighbors.

One of the delights of duck shooting in Czechoslovakia is the opportunity to stay in a hunting castle. Czechoslovakia has the most – and the best-preserved – hunting castles in the world. Some of these are: Orlik, Konopiste, Ohrada, and Hluboká. Vast parquet floors are covered with Tabriz and Hamadan and Shiraz carpets, and forty-foot high walls leading up to vaulted ceilings are covered with hundreds of mounted heads of roe deer, wild boar, sheep, fallow deer, and red stag. Huge tapestries depicting hunting scenes adorn the hallways. At dinnertime a whole roast wild boar might be borne into the dining hall and served. Inevitably, there will be roast mallard with bread dumplings and red cabbage and *Palatschinky* and limitless quantities of that wonderful Czech beer.

THE GRAND PASSAGE

The scene changes to the endless steppe of Kazakhstan in Soviet Central Asia, the breadbasket of the Soviet Union. This is the stopping-off grounds for hundreds of thousands of graylag and white-fronted geese on their way to Turkey and India and points south.

The geese roost and rest on and around a lake, which lies inside a sanctuary. The legal hunting area begins about a half-mile from the lake. Each morning at sunrise the geese get up in waves of 500 to 1000 each and head out to the endless wheat fields. There the local shooters await them, cunningly concealed in large piles of wheat straw. Without benefit of decoys or calls, they depend entirely on luck to bring the geese within gunning range. Since the weather is typically sunny and calm, the birds typically fly high, and the shooters' luck is slight. There is a great deal of unmitigated sky-blasting.

Foreign shooters have somewhat better arrangements. They have the benefit of strategically placed pit blinds and a limited number of decoys. Many of them have brought calls. Although the number of decoys is never sufficient to bring in those large flocks of geese, they do suffice to lure singles and doubles and small flocks. Fortunately, there are a *lot* of small flocks.

While hunting under these circumstances, I often wondered how a professional goose-hunting guide from the rice country near Houston, Texas, equipped with hundreds of decoys and many years experience, could do. I intend to find out soon, as I am making all the arrangements. If everything works the way it should, the steppe of Soviet Central Asia will certainly become the greatest goose-hunting land of all.

Of all the lands where I have hunted waterfowl, Egypt is the one that most compellingly calls me back. The weight of sixty centuries of history presses heavily upon the land. Egypt is a land obsessed with death, one whose principal industry is its past. It is a land of tombs, where you don't really begin to live until you die.

All of the waterfowl shooting is concentrated in the Nile Valley and the Nile Delta, never very far from ruins. Some of the best duck

THE GRAND PASSAGE

shooting takes place virtually at the base of the Maydoon Pyramid – which dates from 2600 B.C. – in the Fayyum oasis. In Upper Egypt, right on the outskirts of Luxor, visiting hunters shoot at vast congregations of Egyptian geese among the Valley of the Kings and the Valley of the Queens and the Colossi of Memnon. They hunt from ruin to ruin across the flat face of Egypt.

Norman Mailer – in his remarkable book, *Ancient Evenings* – has best caught the atmosphere of the Egyptian necropolis:

> *From orchards in the distance came a scent of date and fig trees, and the clear refreshment of the vines. The air on this night gave intimations to me of gardens where once I made love. I knew again the smell of rose and jasmine. Far below, by the riverbank, the palms by the shore would be black in outline against the silver water of the river…Now the air was heavy with the odor of mud. That was the*

aroma of these lands, mud and barley, sweat and husbandry...I thought of tombs, and of friends in tombs. Like the plucking of a heavy string came the first intimation of sorrow.

In a score years of shooting waterfowl around the world certain memories stand out: watching vast constellations of graylag geese, newly arrived from Siberia, pour through the Himalayan passes of the Vale of Kashmir, India; returning with a satisfying load of pintails and teal from a morning shoot on the coastal lagoons of Sinaloa, Mexico, to eat on shore a bucket of steamed clams with lime juice and wash them down with cold Bohemia beer; waiting in a blind and hearing from far across Lake Ikkiyad in Lower Egypt the *muezzin* calling the faithful to prayer at first light; and tracking twisting mallards in a driving wind and rainstorm at Frisenborg Estate, Denmark, and having my best day of mallard shooting ever.

In the words of George Orwell: "Such, such, were the joys."

Terry Wieland, a Canadian, is known for his magazine writing and his books on fine wildlife and sporting artists. So it is only fitting that he should take a look at "The Other Side of Sport," and our fixation with the nuances and memorabilia of waterfowling.

Terry's lighthearted essay on "collectibles" chronicles waterfowlers – and non-waterfowlers alike – and their adventures into decoys, prints, and "ducks on highball glasses" that delight us so.

CHAPTER SEVEN

The Other Side of Sport

by
Terry Wieland

"I get my ducks at Longchamps on Madison Avenue," the surgeon said. "It's air-conditioned in the summer and it's warm in the winter and I don't have to get up before first light and wear long-horned underwear."
"All right, City Boy. You'll never know."

Ernest Hemingway
Across the River and into the Trees

Along about the early 1980s, a new fashion began to manifest itself upon the American scene. Suddenly, in the midst of such inoffensive activities as wiping your feet, hanging up your coat, taking a sip from a highball glass, or even admiring the maiden next door, you were likely to find yourself face to face with a mallard drake.

The phenomenon was known in the fashion world as *duck motif*.

THE GRAND PASSAGE

Where before doormats had read "Welcome," coat hooks were wooden pegs stuck into a board, drinking glasses wore etched flowers, and maidens' T-shirts were graced with tiny alligators, now all were replaced by ducks. Mallard drakes and hens, hooded mergansers, the odd canvasback for the *cognoscenti*, and assorted pintails, widgeons, and goldeneyes found themselves to be the fashion statement of a new decade.

The first glimmer of this trend can be found in the next-to-last catalogue ever issued by the original Abercrombie & Fitch of New York, a famous hunting and fishing store. There, on page 31, is a fiberglass mailbox of the kind that now lines the back lanes of New Jersey, with the family name enlivened by – well, in that illustration, it's a pair of cardinals, but the box also came with pheasant, quail, or mallard. Before too long, however, the mallard was king.

Other catalogues devoted page after page to consumer goods made attractive by the ducks painted, stitched, embroidered, etched, and carved therein and thereon. Nestled among the more pedestrian items – the glasses, the doormats, the coat rack – are often telephones carved and painted in the shape of mallard drakes. When there is an incoming call, some of them even quack.

Walk into any reasonably prosperous, young-to-middle-age household of the 1990s, and chances are you will encounter ducks in some manifestation. It could be the obligatory antique decoy on the mantel; it could be a pair of brass mallard heads holding up the row of unsullied leatherbound books; somewhere, somehow, there will be ducks. *Duck motif*, however, is not just for the trendy. At the Farmers' Co-operative store in Sutton, Ontario, they sell large circular barn thermometers whose faces are painted in different patterns. They have whitetails and pheasants, a Holstein cow and a mallard drake. They sell more mallards, they tell me, than all the others put together.

The spell of ducks has been cast wide. It crosses many boundaries. It includes those who hunt, but also many, many more who do not hunt, have never hunted, and even vehemently oppose hunting. The question is, of course, why? Attractive though they are, mallards are not as graceful as the whitetail, not as exciting as the ruffed grouse, not as compelling as the elk. And yet, they have a following among non-sportsmen that far outstrips any other bird or animal. Why?

On October 19, 1985, at an auction of Americans at Christie's in New York, a pair of antique red-breasted merganser decoys carved by Lothrop Holmes brought a then-record price of $93,500. The event caused headlines, but it was just one of many such in a year that raised eyebrows among decoy collectors, and also among those who observe with awe the prices paid by collectors for items which they themselves would more than likely throw out.

Earlier that same year, at an auction in Hyannisport, a golden plover carved by Bill Bowman brought $50,000 – a single-decoy record; just minutes later, the same buyer paid $39,000 for another Bowman plover. Altogether, decoy sales at formal auctions topped

$3.75 million in 1985, more than twice the previous record of $1.7 million set the year before. Sales of antique decoys were fast earning their way off the classified pages and into the financial section. The prices continue to rise.

By the mid-1980s, any chunk of wood with knife marks that vaguely resembled a feathered creature was being sold in "Antiques & Collectibles" emporia for roughly 9,000 times its real value as firewood. "It's an antique," the hawkers cooed, as customers gingerly surveyed from all angles a crudely hacked and still more crudely painted "decoy," seeking (usually in vain) a perspective from which it would look attractive sitting on the mantel. More often than not, they bought. Better safe than sorry, and it *might* be worth real money.

For actual use, of course, real wooden decoys had long since gone the way of the passenger pigeon. Few people carved decoys any more, and those who did, did so for the mantel-piece trade; duck hunters themselves used the hollow plastic, store-bought, mechanically painted objects which resemble a duck the way a carrousel pony resembles a horse. Which is to say, they don't. While the antique decoy market – both genuine and bogus – was burgeoning, decoy carving by modern master carvers was becoming an art form. They were still called decoys, but they bore as much resemblance to a real decoy as a modern Olympic javelin bears to a hoplite war spear.

These masterpieces of the carver's art – and they are masterpieces – now sell for two or three or five thousand dollars. They have long since entered the realm of decadence, in the obscure sense of that word in which articles are so finely wrought and ornate as to be useless for their original purpose. Decoy carving exhibitions and shows are now divided and subdivided into endless classes according to carving level, subject matter, and manner of rendering. Just one among many is the "working decoy" class, in which the carved article might, in someone's wildest dreams, actually serve the purpose for which it was intended.

Most, however, are not even called decoys any more. They are carvings, or three-dimensional art, and wildfowl are not the only subject matter by any means. You now find grouse and pheasant, hawks and eagles, and even songbirds on a branch or on the wing. And yet, the lure remains the duck, carved in classic form, as in a decoy or a real duck sitting on water. No matter: A decoy by any other name remains a decoy, and the lure of the decoy, for people as for its own kind, is as strong now as ever, and the masters of songbird carving can only sit on the outside looking in, wondering what in heaven's name is the attraction?

And then there are the paintings.

On canvas as in wood, ducks cast a magnetic spell over hunter and non-hunter alike. No wildlife artist has truly arrived, it seems, until he or she has done ducks. This can probably be traced to that most powerful force in wildlife art, the duck stamp competition. These began as a rather informal contest to design a Federal duck stamp; the stamp was then sold to hunters, and the funds derived from them were directed to conservation efforts. Soon, the states were issuing their own duck stamps, designed by the winners in local contests. And before long, of course, the designs were being issued as limited edition prints. Winning a Federal duck stamp competition became the road to fame and semi-fortune for wildlife artists. At the same time, the collecting of the stamps led to vast increases in value, and soon stamps that had sold originally for a couple of dollars were changing hands for a couple of thousand.

The whole duck-art industry, including stamps, limited edition prints, and even originals, continued to grow. Where in 1970, there were eight (8!) art dealers in all of the United States specializing in wildlife art, by the mid-1980s there were more than 1,000. In 1970, there was estimated to be 1,000 collectors of duck stamps and prints; by the mid-'80s, there were 20,000 prints produced from each Federal duck stamp, and still there were not enough to go around.

Duck art has long been a mainstay of the school of painting in which the more a painting resembles a photograph, the more the buyers seem to like it. Interpretation has given way to replication, and thousands upon thousands of duck prints lie under beds in shrink-wrapped splendor, awaiting the day their proud possessors

Pintails High
Courtesy of Mr. and Mrs. Earl Burke

will haul them out and get them framed.

A revealing story: Guy Coheleach, the New Jersey artist and big-game hunter, once did a loose, impressionistic painting of a Siberian tiger in motion, and then browbeat his publisher into issuing it as a print despite the work of artists such as German impressionist Manfred Schatz (impressionistic prints do not, by tradition, sell well). Immediately beset by self-doubt, Coheleach felt the need to show the wildlife art world that he had not lost his marbles and elected to do this by painting a tightly detailed portrait of a bird. He chose as his subject the ever-popular mallard, and proceeded to create "Mallards," a vignette of three mallards in various stages of flight. The work became one of his best-known and most popular paintings; Cohealeach, naturally, has mixed emotions about the whole affair.

It does, however, tell you something about art, the art world, art buyers, and particularly, buyers of *wildlife* art. Ducks sell. Simple as that, and the more realistic, evidently the better.

The annual fund-raising dinner for Ducks Unlimited in New York City is a gathering that ranks with fund-raisers for the Metropolitan Opera. Draped in stylish finery, the Faithful gather to glide around the ballroom of the Ritz and spend money on behalf of waterfowl. Looking around the room, it is hard to picture many of them clad in stained camo in a duck blind; for that matter, it is hard to picture many of them closer to a duck than to infusions of *duck a l'orange*. But there they are. Supporting Ducks Unlimited has become *de rigeur* in these duck-mad days, for corporations and individuals alike. Sporting the distinctive duck profile that is DU's trademark shows the world that you care about the environment.

Ducks Unlimited is North America's oldest, best-known, most widely supported, and by far most successful and powerful conservation organization devoted to the preservation of one species. Ducks Unlimited has grown so far beyond its origin as a banding-together of duck hunters to preserve their favorite prey, most non-hunters today are surprised to learn the organization even has a connection with, much less supports, the hunting of waterfowl. Ducks Unlimited is no longer just a conservation organization; it is a symbol of conservation, of concern, of getting together to do something. If the modern interest in ducks is symbolic, then Ducks Unlimited has become the symbol of a symbol.

Artist Thomas Aquinas Daly of upstate New York is a painter in watercolors and, of late, in oils whose favorite subjects include fly fishing and duck hunting. Which does not make him unique, by any means; what might make him unique is his absolute devotion to tradition and to doing things in traditional ways.

In his part of the country, duck hunting means sneak-boating, an arcane approach in which one man in a sneak-boat, a craft which resembles nothing so much as a scaled-down Atlantic fishing dory, hides behind a screen and allows the boat to drift or blow downwind toward a flock of setting ducks. When the ducks flush, the hunter stands in the boat to shoot. As practiced on Lake Erie, in the dead of late fall with the wind whipping frozen particles of water against your face and your fingertips turning interesting shades of red and purple in the cold, sneak-boating is a pastime whose attraction is lost even on most other duck hunters, much less the population at large.

Daly's devotion to doing things the old way, and doing them himself, has led him not only to build his own sneak-boat, but also to carve his own decoys. As a carver, he is a great watercolorist, and yet his experience with his string of "working" decoys is that they look like a duck to another duck, to use Robert Ruark's phrase, and that is more important than looking like a duck to a duck hunter. They have the rounded forms, the suggested detail, the understatement of the turn-of-the-century decoy masters – nothing at all like the decoys that are displayed each year at carving exhibitions around the continent. When not in use, they lie in a heap in a corner of Daly's barn.

One early December day, in the midst of the late 1980s duck population crash, I had agreed to join Tom Daly for a sneak-boating expedition on Lake Erie. It came to naught because of a sudden southern Ontario frozen rain onslaught that left roads half a foot deep in slush and the ditches overcrowded with vehicles. I telephoned my apologies, to be met with such obvious regret on the other end of the line that I felt overwhelmingly guilty at disappointing a man I greatly admire.

"Well, you know, I am disappointed," Daly said in his extremely direct way. "I was really looking forward to getting out there. We probably wouldn't have seen anything, a day like this. But hell! It would have been great to be out there."

> "It's not just an <u>ordinary</u> duck, you know –
> "It happens to be a <u>wild</u> duck..."
>
> Henrik Ibsen
> *The Wild Duck*

There is another magic to ducks that few but hunters know in this age, and that is the magic of eating ducks.

In the late 1900s, in the era of the market-gunner, non-hunting gourmets could find wild duck on the menu of any self-respecting hotel or restaurant in any big city in America. No one would dream of eating domestic duck when canvasback could be had, done up the equal of any dish prepared by Escoffier.

In one of his later stories about his grandfather, Robert Ruark describes an expedition taken by the Old Man and the Boy to the city of Baltimore, where the Old Man introduces his grandson to certain things about which a man should know.

Ruark shared with Hemingway the ability to describe food in simple and loving detail, almost with awe, as only a man who has experienced serious hunger can describe food. Neither should be read if you are on a diet or on the wagon. And in a piece called "Terrapin Stew Costs Ten Bucks A Quart," Ruark revels in his description of food the way it used to be, and the way it no longer was even in the late 1920s:

THE GRAND PASSAGE

> *The waiter brought the terrapin stew, so hot it bubbled in the dish, and I won't even try to describe what can be done with butter, terrapin eggs, sherry, Jersey cream, and clear terrapin meat. Then the waiter brought in a brace of canvasback. "These powerful unusual* chicken, *boss," he said...*

And the Old Man:

> *They fed you breasts of canvasback duck with stripes of red ham, and from there you went to the brandy and the cigars. I say canvasbacks, because you could buy a brace of four-pounders for two bits. It would have been an insult to feed guests anything but cans, unless mebbe once in a while pintail. But now you're hard put to find a canvasback. The meat gunners shot 'em out because they were so popular.*

And that was in the 1920s.

Of course, in the 1920s, wildlife populations of many kinds were at or near all-time lows. Out West, millions of pronghorns had been reduced to thousands, and millions of bison to hundreds. In some parts of the East, even whitetails were barely hanging on. But the most noticeable decline was in waterfowl populations. Where once the flocks had darkened the sun, now the sun blazed down on ponds undisturbed by the splashing of birds. Hunters blamed the market-gunners, of course, and most people just blamed hunting in general, failing to make the connection between the canvasback they wolfed down in the local hotel, and the dearth of canvasbacks to be found along the riverbanks.

In 1918, the U.S.-Canada migratory bird treaty put an end to market gunning; it also (in theory) put an end to roast canvasback in elegant hotels. Today, how many non-hunters have ever tasted the glories of pintail or canvasback properly prepared? Still, the words "roast duck" evoke an instant vision of succulence, and it ain't duck out of a farmer's yard, either.

Walk into any house early in this century, in country or in town, and you would find somewhere behind the door, in the back of a closet, over a fireplace – a shotgun bearing a name like "Iver Johnson," "Champion," or "Excel." Some would be doubles, side-by-sides, plain boxlock affairs; others would be singles, simple break-open guns with half-pistol grip, external hammer, and a 30 or 32-inch barrel choked tighter than a Christmas turkey on December 24th. All would have beat-up wood stocks and bluing turned to a rusty brown patina from years of handling in bad weather. Such guns were made for waterfowling – were of little use for anything else, in fact, except possibly turkey hunting. They were built for duck blinds, and looked out of place anywhere else. Even men who hunted nothing else hunted ducks, it seemed.

With the advent of closed seasons came that heretofore unknown phenomenon, Opening Day, and Opening Day of duck season has a lure all its own. Where I grew up, you could tell Opening Day because it was always a Saturday, and you awoke that Saturday morning to the far-off boom of shotguns. On toward mid-morning, the hunters would come trundling in, wet, muddy, dragging a few decoys, and some, a few ducks. The birds would be laid out at the end of the driveway, partly to get them out of the way while the car was unloaded, but mostly to give the neighbors and passers-by a chance to stop and admire them.

Duck hunting is the most peculiarly North American of all hunting activities. The various upland game pursuits have their slightly distorted mirror image in Europe; all big-game hunting has its counterpart in Europe, in Africa, or in Asia. And while waterfowl are hunted by small enclaves of Europeans in the inland marshes of Spain, in the salt marshes off the south coast of England, and along the bitter Baltic coast, nowhere is there duck hunting – nor has there ever been – to compare with the duck hunting to be had in North America during the so-called Golden Age of Shotgunning.

The die-hard waterfowling Europeans could only look with unbelieving envy at the wealth the North American shotgunner was blessed with, virtually by walking down to the nearest piece of damp real estate and settling in. An while hunting in North America was and is, by European standards, a decidedly democratic activity, duck hunting rather quickly became the most exclusive form of hunting, with the possible exception of plantation quail hunting in the South.

Private hunt clubs were formed, and vast acreages of wetlands were posted, for the exclusive use of the members. Writers like Nash Buckingham told the story of this kind of hunting to those who could not experience it, and his works are classics.

Shotgun manufacturers like Parker, L.C. Smith, Lefever, Ithaca, and Fox catered to the tastes of all with shotguns that ranged from the utilitarian to the Utopian. It is possible to gauge the temper of those times from the shotguns that are available on the used-gun market today. You are more likely by far to find a 12-gauge, 30-inch barreled, tightly choked Parker, Ithaca, Fox, or L.C. Smith than any other gauge, length, or configuration. Waterfowl guns outsold all others. Where, in poorer or less committed households, you would find an Iver Johnson or a Champion, in the more upscale establishments, you would find an Ithaca or a Parker.

An old A.H. Fox ad from before the Depression tells it all: "And this is my first year of gunning," says the proud owner of a Fox shotgun, standing on a porch overlooking a duck marsh, with a brace of ducks in one hand and his shotgun in the other. The gun is being admired by two friends, and all three are wearing ties. The key work, of course, is "gunning." There were so many ducks, it was not a question of whether you would get your limit, but of how quickly, and whether they would be the desirable canvasbacks, pintails, and mallards.

And everyone did it, it seemed. If not your father, then certainly your grandfather, or an uncle. The legend of the "hunting uncle" is as much a piece of North American family folklore as the inept brother-in-law. My father, to the best of my knowledge, never hunted anything at all after he came back from the war at the age of twenty-nine, and before that, only rabbits (with ferrets) and ducks. But to the day of his death he always kept his old Excel 12-gauge single, and the sight of ducks in flight or on a distant bay would always move him to gaze after them.

He never took me duck hunting, but when I was fifteen he handed the old Excel into my keeping. It was not a gift – more on the order of a loan. And even now, I do not think of it is *my* shotgun. It is unapologetically a gun of the "Long Tom" variety – good for passing shots on ducks and geese, and not much else. It is a link with my father, a man for whom I had little understanding until long after his death. As I get older, I get to know him better. But of course, it is long since too late for it to do any good.

The Golden Age of Shotgunning, if it ever really existed, is long gone; what Michael McIntosh calls the Golden Age of Remembering is very much with us. Soon, we may not have much else.

Ernest Hemingway, in a postscript to *A Farewell to Arms*, which Maxwell Perkins excised before the book was printed, wrote a line to the effect that, "You never really have anything until you lose it."

It is almost certain that duck hunters of the 1890s never thought they were living in the Golden Age. If anything, they probably bemoaned the passing of the Good Ol' Days just as we do. Now *their* days are the good ol' days, the Golden Age, and it lives on for us through a badly worn Excel single shot 12-gauge, or a cracked and brittle decoy sitting on a mantelpiece, or a print of mallards in flight, numbered and signed by the artist. To our eternal sorrow, by Hemingway's measure, we now truly have waterfowling, because in many ways, we have truly lost it, at least the way it once was.

And so we troop to auction houses to bid on antique decoys of questionable intrinsic worth, but incalculable symbolic value. We haunt used-goods stores, searching for duck-hunting paraphernalia and hang it beside the mantelpiece like an amulet. We buy paintings of ducks, and carvings of ducks, and place them about the house – icons that remind us not of hunting we have done or would like to do, but as a link with the past of our fathers.

There is a certain cultural continuity to be had by scattering ducks around us in varied forms, whether they be ducks on the doormat, mallards on the mail box, greenwings on glasses, or canvasback coat racks. Of course, if you asked anyone why they had ducks like these, you would probably get a vague, "I just like ducks." Few, if any, would say they collect them as a means of touching their ancestors' way of life.

As far as I know, no academic has examined the role of the duck in our culture the way anthropologists have studied the bison *vis a vis* the Plains Indians, but I suspect they would find it is of similar value, symbolically if not materially. When the bison disappeared, to all intents and purposes, so did the Indian. Should the duck ever reach similar straits, we would be no less affected. So we must learn to enjoy waterfowl in other ways than "gunning." Our Grand Passage must be to a higher consciousness, the next plane of appreciation.

It seems we are all searching for the same thing: Tom Daly pushing his sneak-boat out into Lake Erie through the breaking December waves; the Long Island suburbanite making his way through Manhattan to the DU dinner; the collector raising his hand at a decoy auction or putting his name in for the limited edition print of this year's duck stamp – all are taking part in a cultural ritual that celebrates a way of life and mourns its passing at one and the same time.

Even John Denver, singing: "I took two shots, got no ducks, and cold, cold hands."

Yeah.

But hell! Wasn't it great to be out there?

If there is a finer outdoor essayist than Gene Hill, he hasn't emerged yet. Hill has proven to be one of the best who has ever written on the feeling of being outdoors, of the total sporting experience.

Nowhere is this more evident than when he writes of waterfowl, particularly geese, which seem to strike a note in him that no other wild creature can. Although he is a world-class game shot, Hill more often is the observer who pulls divergent thoughts and moods into the seamless prose that is his alone as he does here in "The Wild Goose."

CHAPTER EIGHT

The Wild Goose

by
Gene Hill

From the blind sitting with its front feet in the water, I look out over a small pond made a turbid brown by the black paddles of geese, one of the things I do now that I seem pressed for time and short on real places. It's not a real pond, just a shallow, scooped-out cup that will be plowed up for the spring planting. But I like it here, as strange as that may seem for a man who likes, late of an evening, to think of himself as a hunter.

Beyond the pond, no more than half a mile, you can see an old farmhouse, its crumbling brick walls losing their hold on each other – the way old things let go – and gently sliding back into the same clay where they started.

Close to the farmhouse is the skeleton of a clapboard room held together by its chimney spine. They tell me that this was once the township school; I tell them that once I went to a school much like it and they look at me a little odd, but I really did. Like the non-scholar I was, I remember best the sounds of recess and the games we played with no more than a ball and stick and cheered on by the barking of the farm dogs who walked us to school and walked us home and shared our lunches and brought back the balls we batted out of the tiny schoolyard.

I see little flocks of geese, drifting like rising smoke, over the tilted chimney. I know they won't come to a call, but since I'm alone I blow it just the same; the sound of it seems to shove them even farther away, the way good singers, those with pitch, used to edge away from me when I sang in Sunday school.

It's unsettling to see the same geese I just frightened circle low over shopping malls and drop in to graze fields where they feed under harrows and plows left for the winter and quarrel over spilled silage just a few yards from a busy farmyard.

I guess we have something in common about wildness – in one place we are; just a little further on we're not. "My" geese are wild when they're far enough away in the sky to be abstract and my mind is up there with them, not down here listening to the long-ago voices from a barely remembered childhood.

Everything reaches a compromise; neither the geese nor I listen to the sounds of traffic – just to each other as if we're both pretending things are not as they are, but how they ought to be. They're here because this is where they have always been at this time of the year, and I am here because they are.

One of the things I like about hunting is *thinking* about what I'm hunting; to mull the questions I can't answer. I like not knowing how all of a sudden feeding geese, who up until a certain moment have been sharing a tattered cornfield and goose gossip, will suddenly, for no reason I can fathom, stop as one and raise their heads and fly. And not randomly as you and I might run when frightened, in opposite ways, but thoughtfully, purposefully, precisely. And then, just as mysteriously, they'll circle once or twice and land right back where they have just been. Or form a long flared "V," like a giant feather arrowhead, and disappear into nothingness.

I have, just for the "why not" of it, tried walking, bold and noisy, up on a bunch of feeding geese in an open field and several times gotten well into gun range. I have also hidden in a blind so well concealed you'd be hard put to see it until you nearly fell over it, with a spread of a hundred perfectly placed decoys and with an expert caller turning himself blue in the face, and watched flock after flock circle this ideal layout once or twice and then go silently away.

They say you have to be as smart as a goose to take any. I'm not but I have, and I don't really know much more about the whole operation than I ever did, which is one of the reasons I'm out there so often, as innocent of knowledge as a babe, and just as content.

THE GRAND PASSAGE

Maybe something right will happen is about all the heavy thinking I can bring to bear on a day in a goose blind. No different from all the hunters before me and no different, I hope and trust, from all the hunters that will come in future times.

Birds are not gifted with reason and logic; they merely respond with nothing more complicated than simple instinct and its variations of fear and trust. While some of us are more skilled callers than others, so are others more gifted wingshots or more able to sit still and be patient.

I am more than fair when it comes to goose hunting. I violate, knowingly, all the tenets I ought to observe. I fidget, I look up when I shouldn't, I call and I know better; no matter how hard I practice, it sounds like "a cat in a trap," according to one of my guides.

Change the blind to a pit, change the pit to a layout boat, change the boat to a patch of brush. Change the state, change the country. Nothing changes. Geese are geese, thinking goose thoughts. My imagination listens to the honks and gutterals, and I hear the passing of wisdom from the old to the young. I hear the birds of the year saying they're tired or hungry and the leaders telling them, "It's just a little farther and we'll rest." Maybe they sing songs about the places they've come from and places they are anxious to see again. Maybe they just say words of comfort like a parent calming an anxious child or a friend soothing one of the fretful old folks. If only I were smart enough to know.

The goose is a traveler and so am I. I have stood underneath them from tundra to prairie, watching and listening, thinking and wondering. I know they will abandon their young to be cared for by another pair – and once, on my pond, to an old aunt of a white farmyard goose who was obviously so happy with the brood that she talked and played with them day and night.

I think about these things. I think about the fact that they can fly at thirty thousand feet or get along with just one leg and can be quarrelsome to the extreme. They seem to edge back and forth to the edge of humanity – with all its faults and all its nonsense; civilized and cruel. I think of all the places they've taken me – real and unreal – and I don't understand it.

I react to them as a force of nature that intrigues me with its mystery and yet leaves me often with the thought that someday I'll

The Wild Goose

see it all clearly and know better why I have to be here with them...

I tend to daydream. Just before dark, a pair of geese slip into the pond before I see them. They roll and splash, having a recess of their own on this wet edge of the playground of the old schoolyard. Now I decide to wait until they leave of their own accord. They are like a soft hand on my shoulder and I can't bring myself to frighten them.

Other geese are sliding overhead, their calling seems to come from behind the stars – thin and distant and chill. My pond geese pay no attention but this inspires me. Asking silent forgiveness of my friend Jim Olt, I began to honk, doing the very best I know how. The geese stop splashing and look around and unhurriedly but surely begin swimming to the far side. They walk up into the field and disappear into the night.

I pack my stuff and leave the blind and stand for a moment at the edge of the pond. I am tempted to call out into the darkness a lovely thought I remember from Thoreau: *The woods would be very silent if no birds sang except those that sing best.*

But I don't. Why waste a good line when there's no one listening?

Other Titles by Countrysport Press

BEST GUNS by *Michael McIntosh*

THE BIG BORE RIFLE: The Book of Fine Magazine & Double Rifles .375-.700 Caliber by *Michael McIntosh*

CALL OF THE QUAIL: A Tribute to the Gentleman Game Bird

EASTERN UPLAND SHOOTING by *Dr. Charles C. Norris*

GAME SHOOTING: The Definitive Book on the Churchill Method of Instinctive Wingshooting and Sporting Clays by *Robert Churchill and Macdonald Hastings*

"MR. BUCK": The Autobiography of Nash Buckingham by *Nash Buckingham*

RETRIEVER TRAINING: The Cotton Pershall Method by *Bobby N. George, Jr.*

SHOTGUNNER'S NOTEBOOK: The Advice and Reflections of a Wingshooter by *Gene Hill*

The following Countrysport Press titles are also available in DELUXE LIMITED EDITIONS:

BEST GUNS

THE BIG-BORE RIFLE: The Book of Fine Magazine & Double Rifles .375-.700 Caliber

CALL OF THE QUAIL: A Tribute to the Gentleman Game Bird

EASTERN UPLAND SHOOTING

THE GRAND PASSAGE: A Chronicle of North American Waterfowling

"MR. BUCK": The Autobiography of Nash Buckingham

SHOTGUNNER'S NOTEBOOK: The Advice and Reflections of a Wingshooter

The Countrysport limited editions feature:
*deluxe leather binding
*gilt-edged top papers
*ribbon bookmark
*specially commissioned gold foil cover art
*commemorative title page bearing the edition size and volume number with author's signature where applicable